D1759659

Growing Sustainable Children

NEWHAM LIBRARIES

90800101098647

Growing Sustainable Children

A Garden Teacher's Guide

Ronni Sands
&
Willow Summer

SteinerBooks
2017

*The publication of this book was made possible in part
by a grant from the Waldorf Curriculum Fund.*

Published by Lindisfarne Books
an imprint of SteinerBooks
www.steinerbooks.org
610 Main Street
Great Barrington, Massachusetts 01230

ISBN: 978-1-58420-942-3
e-book ISBN: 978-1-58420-943-0

Copyright © 2017 Ronni Sands, Willow Summer

Cover Design by Elena Loke

All Photography by Miguel Salmaron
(except where noted)

All rights reserved. No part of this publication may be reproduced by any
means without the prior written permission of the publisher.

Printed in the United States of America

❧ CONTENTS ❧

Introduction

by Ronni Sands

WHY TEACH CHILDREN TO GARDEN? Our culture today is becoming more and more removed from nature. Our modern fast-paced lives make procuring and eating healthy food a challenge of enormous proportions, far from a natural experience. Eating is a basic human need. Growing food and caring for the earth is primal. It follows that the more we engage children with this practice, the more they have an opportunity to perceive the world of nature and their role in her care. Immersing ourselves in the rhythms of the seasons—something that happens naturally through caring for a garden—can rekindle a lost relationship and empower children to take responsibility for their own nourishment and food choices. The purpose of this book is to nurture this interrelationship of children, gardens, and preparing food.

When I observe children in a garden, I see that they intuitively know what to do. They are gentle with plants, love to dig in the soil, and carefully place the roots of plants in the earth. They love to bring water to the newly planted seedlings and, of course, they love to eat! When they harvest the fruits and vegetables they have grown, then cutting, cooking, and eating becomes a sacred act. They are truly nourished.

For more than twenty-five years I have been teaching gardening to children and adolescents. Over the years, through observation and practice, I have created a curriculum that is based on a picture of child development used in Waldorf schools. The curriculum builds on itself through the grades, adding new skills, concepts and abilities year after year.

In writing this book I hope to give guidance to teachers and parents on how to build a gardening program that is fitting for their school or home setting and, at the same time, places the curriculum in an age-appropriate context. Through trial and error, I have gained a deep understanding and appreciation of how Waldorf education, based on the educational philosophy of Rudolf Steiner, enriches the child's imagination, stimulates the intellect, and provides a curriculum rich in artistic values. In the garden, over a child's educational journey, each lesson meets the child at his own stage of development.

We are facing an environmental crisis. Crisis is good because it brings us to consciousness. This awakening has already begun and, increasingly, schools are recognizing a need for gardening and outdoor education. What we give time to becomes important. Having a regular time of the day when children work with and experience nature represents a path out of this crisis. To have a lasting impact, ecological principles must be woven into all aspects of education as experiences as well as concepts. Big or small, urban or rural, a space for a garden can lead children back to the natural world. If we want our children to have access to the many resources in nature, we must educate them to love and preserve these resources. This is the first step in building a heart-felt relationship to nature and growing "sustainable children."

Our Different Roles

Co-authorship is a marriage of minds and hearts. I met Willow, a long-time farmer, teacher, and author, when she came to do student teaching at the Summerfield Farm. I asked her if she knew anyone who could type a manuscript, since I was interested in making my ideas gleaned from years of teaching available. Thus began our collaboration. Willow and I have each contributed in a circular fashion. The process has been: I write, Willow types and brings questions and suggestions, and then we are on to the next draft. This book has been a five-year work in-progress and an act of love. In the same way a teacher learns most from her students, a writer learns most from her co-author. Willow excels with form, structure and technology. These are skills I lack. I have a flowing pen and file folders brimming with articles and notes, lesson plans and information. Together we married our talents to give rise to this useful book. In addition to the collaborative writing of the manuscript, I credit Willow for her work on the introduction to biodynamics and the nursery and kindergarten chapter. Without her, the book wouldn't have been possible. That she was able to translate my messy chicken scratch and bring it into form is a miracle of huge proportions.

How to Use this Book

The chapter entitled "The Child's Changing Consciousness" gives a window into the child's physical, emotional, and soul development. The later chapters will give more specific indications for practical application including curriculum, site development, and a variety of activities for each grade. When these hands-on experiences are merged with the pedagogical understanding of the child at a particular age, "growing sustainable children" becomes a spiritual undertaking for the teacher.

As in all of life, teachers must carve their own path. We all have talents, interests, and specialties that can be adapted and expanded. What you already know and love in relationship to gardening will be a rich resource for your own curriculum development. The possibilities are limitless. Let this book be a springboard for your own creativity, not a prescription.

May your children's spirits grow in healthy soil.

The Foundations of Garden Teaching

1 Essential Concepts

Gardening is an active participation in the mysteries of the universe. By gardening, our children learn that they constitute with all growing things a single community of life. They learn to nurture and be nurtured in a universe that is always precarious but ultimately benign. They learn profound reasons for the seasonal rituals of the greatest religious traditions.

—*Thomas Berry*

A HEALTHY GARDEN is vibrant with activity. In spring, this liveliness can be seen in the bursting of buds, the sprouting of seeds, and the leafing of trees. Rudolf Steiner called these unseen forces "life forces" or "etheric forces." They work to orient and strengthen the physical element and require nourishment in order to function properly. The fact that these forces are unseen does not mean that they do not exist. In young children, healthy life forces are seen in their rosy, full cheeks, their active play, and their boundless wills. How we keep these forces abundant in children is similar to how we nourish the vitality of our garden plants. With sufficient water, nutrients, and care, our garden thrives; with sufficient rest, rhythm, and nourishment, the children thrive.

Repetition and Routine

How can this inherent vitality in children be maintained? In repetition children find strength. Routines and simplicity provide a foundation from which children can grow, develop, explore and investigate, free from the anxiety of wondering, "What will come next?"

The basic rhythm of our own breath guides us in forming children's activities. An in-breath (taking in and absorbing) is always followed by an out-breath (relaxing and releasing into the environment). A garden lesson starts with a verse or a story. This is the first concentrating "in-breath." The work activity that day is the releasing "out-breath." Coming together at the end of the lesson and sharing a snack or a verse is the final "in-breath." The children can then transition back to the classroom in a state of equilibrium. A lack of breathing in the lesson can result in stress that manifests in exhaustion, hyperactivity, or emotional outbursts.

Healthy rhythms for children's lives reflect the earth's great rhythms. The seasons give a picture of the cycles of wakeful activity in spring and summer, and quiet rest in fall and winter. A child's day should mirror these natural rhythms with periods of doing and rest; of indoors and outdoors; of academic and artistic time. Sunrise and sunset form a structure for waking and sleeping. Creating stable daily, weekly, and yearly rhythms for children builds their life forces and allows them to relax into a routine they can trust. When the form of a gardening lesson is repeated the children can relax and engage more deeply.

Seasonal celebrations give form to the year and let children know nature is an integral part of life. Being connected to this great rhythm nourishes children's life forces. Human physiology is deeply tied to earthly rhythms. For example, flying into a different time zone disrupts sleep. The cycle of the year is the in-breath and out-breath of the earth itself. The fall brings the harvest celebration: a time of abundance and thanksgiving. Putting the garden beds to sleep by clearing and mulching is a preparation for the coming winter when the days grow shorter and darker and the growing cycle pauses. In winter the earth is less active above the surface. During this period we let her rest and rebuild, much like the child replenishes during sleep. In spring, when the earth is awakened, seeds are planted and the journey begins again. Summer, filled with warmth, sun and growth, is the great out-breath.

We are truly dependent on the earth's natural processes. Our civilization has developed to a point where we can ignore many of the earth's natural rhythms. For example, electric lights and heat allow the same levels of activity in winter as in summer. If we ignore these rhythms in the garden, however, we will not succeed. Paying attention to the earth's rhythms and seasons and their different qualities and necessities allows students to deeply internalize their dependence on the earth.

The Four Elements

The garden is a natural place to teach about the elements that combine in a myriad of ways to create the world around us. In high school a more complex view based on the periodic table of elements is introduced in classroom work. This is possible due to their capacity for abstract thinking and ability to use scientific tools and concepts. In the earlier grades, the basic elements of earth, water, air, and fire, which can be perceived directly with the senses, can be brought in developmentally appropriate ways. These so-called elements can be seen in different parts of the plant, though they are never in isolation. For example, the watery quality of the stem, the warmth in the oils of herb flowers, the strong root of an oak tree in the earth.

In early childhood, telling stories that involve nature spirits helps paint lively pictures of what earth provides for roots, water for leaves, air for blossoms, and fire for seeds. Weather and plant growth is brought about by "Mother earth," "Father sun," "Sister rain" and "Brother wind," creating a picture of familial interdependence. Such images must feel personally relevant and true for each teacher. They can be brought through any of the world traditions or creatively developed on the spot.

As children grow older, the role of the elements can be developed in a more concrete way as they explore the many aspects and interrelationships of each element in the growth of the garden. By introducing the four elements in imaginative and concrete ways, children develop a sense for the unseen elements that form our earthly basis for survival. The role of the human being, with the inherent capacity to order the elements through conscious thought and action, can be considered the "fifth element"—"*quinta essentia*"—equally as important as the other four. Bringing an active consciousness to bear on the natural world in a healthy way completes the picture of the gardening curriculum in the later years.

When children work with natural processes, they are gaining an instinctive feeling for nature that allows them to make proper judgments in later life. There is lawfulness in nature that can be seen in daily gardening activities. Direct experience creates a sensitivity and understanding that can't be found in a book; it is a discernment that they know with their whole body. When children care for a piece of land, they make a connection that lives forever. The ability for fingers to discern how deep to plant the seed, or place the roots in the ground, results from this ongoing exposure to the natural world. This teaches good judgment that can extend to all areas of life.

Picture Consciousness: Imitation and Imagination

Young children are imitative beings up until the age of six or seven. Their primary and most healthy mode of learning is through imitation. They take in what they observe without filters and work it through in their play much like the digestion of food. Play is the most accessible means for understanding the world. Impressions are a form of food that can be healthy and nourishing, or taxing to the system by making it difficult for them to overcome impressions that they cannot digest. What they can digest, they can make their own. Before the change of teeth, around the age of seven, children live in a dream-like state of consciousness and are influenced by the actions and intentions of the adults. Words and explanations have little impact. Their world is not a world of concepts, but one of pictures drawn from their environment. Our actions show our intentions and the child imitates this truth, not by following what we say, but by imitating what we do. In the garden we can best meet the child's consciousness with stories, verses, songs, games, and meaningful work—all of which work through images and actions rather than explanations.

Garden teaching that stimulates the imagination brings vitality to children's actions and provides fertile ground for learning. When speaking in the garden, the inner pictures being held by the teacher strongly influence the children's experience. In developing the capacity for abstract thinking, adults have left behind their picture-making ability. In order to meet the children where they are, we have to consciously re-create the pictures in our minds to make them vivid for our students. Do you picture the sun when you speak of the sunflower? If so, you are speaking their language and allowing children to create their own internal pictures. Each activity can be described metaphorically. When planting seeds we can be gnomes burying their treasure. Each class can begin with a story that relates to the day's activity and brings the children towards the lesson in their own imaginative picturing. For example, for the activity of planting corn, beans, and squash, begin with a story about the "Three Sisters" from Native American lore.

Stories have been used as educational tools throughout history in all cultures, teaching universal truths and allowing children to find their place in the world through symbol and archetype. Universal pictures, or archetypes, such as the ones found in the garden in the processes of the growth, development, and decay of plants, or the activity of small animals and birds preparing for winter, teach powerful lessons. Nature becomes alive with meaning. Meeting the children in their picture consciousness, rather than teaching them static concepts of a more scientific nature, supports the healthy development of life forces.

A sixth grade class may begin with a verse by Dorothy Harrar, which provides the image that enables the students to picture the real work of their gardening classes. This verse gives the picture that each seed that is tucked into the earth holds an entire plant within it. It also draws the children towards the archetypal plant growth process that mirrors their own development.

> *Invisibly within the seed,*
> *The plant is waiting for its day of birth.*
> *Root, stem and leaf, the flower and fruit*
> *Will sprout and bloom and ripen.*
> *As the sun and rain call them forth,*
> *So life will call from me what now is invisibly waiting.*

Weaving concepts into the pictorial elements lays the groundwork for the development of thinking. The pictures from this poem come alive as one observes, after a few weeks, how the squash or pumpkin plants have pushed their way out of the seed. On the edge of the leaf of this newly birthed plant hangs the seed coat. One can witness that the plant lives, first within the seed, and then, outside of it.

The poem is an example of directly observing, witnessing, and imagining the stages of growth in a plant. Holding this picture in our imagination creates an opportunity to respect and revere the forces that are active both in us and in plants.

Observation as a Tool for Developing Intellectual Capacities

As we engage in farm work with adolescents, they become active participants in the life processes taking place on the farm. To do the farm and garden work well, one must constantly be watching and observing growth processes. The environment stimulates a whole host of questions: What does the plant need? Is this a weed? Where should I prune? How far apart should the plants be? Is the plant getting enough water, light, air? The children gradually learn to sense the life forces in the natural world. Through this witnessing, the students begin to form an inner imagination of plants as they grow in time and space. This ability to imagine is a guide to the actual physical work: without these ordered inner pictures, the apparent chaos of nature remains impenetrable and impossible to work with. This approach from imagination to observation to conceptualization gives a wholeness to the thinking of the developing adolescent.

The teaching of concepts becomes more appropriate at later developmental stages, reaching a culmination in high school. Characterizing what we can observe in nature leads to further exploration, questions, and, eventually, to true concepts; while leading with definitions halts the process of inquiry and can stifle the imagination. We want to stimulate student's questions and see what conclusions they can arrive at without providing all the answers.

Meeting the Child Developmentally

It is important to approach all education developmentally. When children are asked to do tasks beyond their capacity a sacrifice must be made in their growth. For instance, when children are required to think abstractly before the age of seven, they use the forces of vitality that should be busy at work building their physical bodies and sustaining their will activity. Instead of being "healthy peaches," they become "dried fruit." When children have been allowed to build these forces, vitality is seen in their face. These same forces will later be used for abstract thought.

Each task in the life of the garden can be understood as suitable for specific ages. How does one look at the unlimited possibilities for farm and garden work as well as experiences in nature, and creatively decide which task fits with what age? Understanding each stage and matching it with the appropriate activity is an ongoing study and practice. When children are given a project that meets them developmentally, presented with imagination and inspiration, they will naturally find love for their work. This engagement fosters a love of the earth with no need to talk about it. Children have an innate kinship with nature that can be properly cultivated or prematurely drained by scientific or abstract lessons. Children who live prematurely in a world of abstract ideas are robbed of the ability to easily engage their will with the activity brought by the teacher. Children who talk incessantly without working need more help to enter into their will and leave behind the abstract. Imagination is a key to help these children realign their will with the work in the garden.

Nurturing the Senses

For the young child, the senses are a gateway to the world. The five senses are tools for exploring and fully experiencing the garden. Is a leaf smooth or fuzzy? Are the birds singing? Can I hear the hum of the bee? Does the smell of the lemon balm lift my spirit? Does the taste of the sorrel pucker my tongue? We work to feed but not overwhelm the senses. Because children are open, yet unable to distinguish good sense experiences from bad, we must educate ourselves and hold this awareness on their behalf. For example, singing to children is calming, while listening to recorded music that is appropriate for adults can be over-stimulating and lead to exhaustion. Taking the time to pause and have a real sense experience is more important than rushing through the work to be done. Becoming aware of how children's senses are affected by their environment is a first step in creating healthy, age-appropriate learning environments.

Physical and Social Life Forces

The work of gardening strengthens the students' life forces by engaging the activity of the heart, the muscles, and the breath. They have an innate drive to develop their physical abilities through movement. Gardening, games, and movement classes provide a healthy outlet for this natural instinct. The children find their own rhythm and strength in digging, cultivating, shoveling, and transplanting. These large motor activities provide the out-breath in a lesson. Nutrition is an important part of building healthy life forces. Food serves to replenish and rebuild, and connects the students with one of the purposes of gardening and farming: supplying our daily bread.

There is a social quality that must develop in order for everyone to work together on one garden plot. As the children find their place in a community project, give-and-take, sharing, caring, listening, and being inclusive are necessary. A garden is a place where social intelligence and empathy for others can develop. The gardening teacher orchestrates physical work that calls upon students to work together cooperatively, actively giving guidance and suggestions for navigating conflicts while allowing all students their perspective. Gardening is a social art where we create visual beauty for others that we couldn't do alone.

Holistic Garden Teaching

All members of an ecological community are interconnected in a vast and intricate network of relationships, the web of life. They derive their essential properties and, in fact, their very existense from their relationships to other things.—Fritjof Capra

Teaching from the whole to the parts is an underpinning of Waldorf pedagogy. Instead of starting with separate facts or ideas, start with the whole and proceed through to the details. Strive to place each lesson or activity within a complete context. This highlights the essential interdependence of all life and shows the children a picture of the world and their place in it. When ideas are presented in isolation a healthy wholeness is lacking. For example, if we start a lesson by measuring root growth, we take the plant out of the context of its environment that includes soil, sun, water and air, all of which contribute to its root development.

This simple difference has great implications in regard to students' ability to acquire truly logical and moral thinking as they mature. Although the whole and the parts are both essential in any process, the parts lose meaning when not viewed as interdependent. We can see the results of an improper order in our modern world when countless scientific advancements—each, if taken individually, seemingly helpful— add up to a way of life that is endangering our survival in the natural environment. Rather than starting at a young age to teach scientific principals about nature—which can unfortunately have the effect of frightening or causing hopelessness—we foster an innate sense for ecological balance by starting from the whole over and over again through the years. Taught the inherent balance that lives in nature, called "the web of life," children have a picture of wholeness. At a later age when students learn about the imbalances created by humans, they have answers that give solutions because they have learned what the natural balance is. Build the beautiful picture that's inherent in nature and the children will know what really exists in a healthy ecosystem.

Practical activities, especially gardening and farming, are naturally suited to teaching holism not as a concept, but through actually experiencing whole processes—something which has become rare in the educational setting. Our material culture has become increasingly specialized and complicated. Few of us may ever have the opportunity to put together a computer, or be able to replicate all the materials and steps necessary to fabricate a car, but we can milk a cow and make the cream into butter, or grow wheat and bake it with wood fire into a loaf of bread. With these experiences behind them, when students of today begin to contribute their gifts to society, they will be more empowered, more capable, more practical and more likely to take the whole into consideration. Having experiences of how difficult it can be to make something such as a wooden spoon from scratch can also lead to more gratitude for all the work done to produce our modern way of life. In addition, visiting places where the items of daily life are made can help children understand the resources and services that contribute to our comforts and survival.

2 The Child's Changing Consciousness

If a young child has been able in his play to give up his whole living being to the world around him, he will be able, in the serious tasks of later life, to devote himself with confidence and power to the service of the world. —Caroline von Heydebrand

THROUGH THE AGE OF SEVEN, children are still at one with their surroundings. They live in a world of awe and wonder where all "things" are alive. Flowers with an open gesture—dandelion, dahlia, sunflower, and tulip—are good images of the young child's consciousness. These flowers are bursting from the center and they open to take in the periphery.

Within this cosmic unity, children are thirsty to know how everything works. They are most interested in the relationships between living things. For them, everything is alive. When they ask "Why?" they mean, but are unable to put into words, "How are the elements of my world connected?" Young children embody a deep wisdom, and yet still want help understanding their world. Everything in the world *is* interdependent. As we mature we begin to feel more and more separate, and begin to have the experience that elements in our world are inanimate. Young children don't yet have this awareness of separateness. Answers that fit with their limited life experience, yet allow their consciousness to remain in the cosmic unity, are developmentally appropriate and satisfying.

When a child asks, "Why does it rain?" rather than giving an explanation of the water cycle, create a "true" imagination such as the following: "Did you know that

~ 11 ~

the ocean is the rain's mother? Sometimes the rain wants to play with the wind in the sky. But then the wind is a bit rough and cold, so the rain begins to miss his mother. Soon he falls to the earth and rushes down the river and back into his mother's arms." This explanation is true both to the child's life experience (I leave my mother because I want to play at school, but then I miss my mother and am so happy to see her at the end of the day), and to nature. This story does not contradict a scientific picture of the water cycle and gives a satisfying answer to the child.

Given imaginitive, "true" pictures of natural processes in response to children's questions, they begin to understand the forces at work in the world. Their developmentally appropriate sense of the world as a unity is intact.

The elemental, creative forces in nature are introduced into children's play through the teacher's modeling of awe and reverence for the living world. Children will imitate the teacher's gesture. In the classroom and on the nature table, the teacher creates scenes from natural materials. These scenes ennoble these simple objects. Then, children instinctively find and collect treasures from nature and create tiny worlds in their outdoor play.

While thinking lies asleep in the young child, their feeling life is awakened by the attitude of reverence and respect for the environment around them. Words of explanation are most often counterproductive. The gestures, attitudes, and equanimity of the teacher, which reflect their inner sense of right and wrong, contribute to the child's future morality. The children absorb these qualities, and make them their own, trusting the teacher. Instructions about good behavior are futile, as the young child cannot interpret abstract concepts. Instead, give small stories that affirm proper actions with examples.

In the nursery, kindergarten, and first grade, children learn primarily through imitation. Raking, digging, and sweeping channel their will into purposeful, helpful work. The simple act of raking leaves into a pile, first to make order, and then to take the valuable material to the compost pile, all while participating in a rhythmical movement, brings warmth and activates the blood. Accompanying such activities with a song allows them to stay in a dreamy state, while the movements engage their will.

Cultivating the unity of the whole group rather than individual desires begins at this age. The teacher reminds the students that this is "our" flower garden rather than "my" plant. Experiences of working for the good of the group can transform natural selfish drives in a gentle way. We are working against a force in the world that makes us desire ownership and breaks the unity we are trying to support at this age.

Kindergarten and nursery children are still held in the oneness of the class, and move like a herd. Their lessons are play, which for them is work. In first grade the children's awareness becomes focused and individual: they are able to participate in a structured lesson, sit in a desk, and work in small groups. The physical change of loosing the teeth and growing permanent ones is a marker for their developmental readiness for learning.

> *Receive the children in reverence,*
> *Educate them in love,*
> *And send them forth in freedom.*
> *—Rudolf Steiner*

Second Grade Consciousness

Children at this age have a large head in proportion to their body, much like a dandelion, with its large seed-head reaching to the sun. The second grader is building confidence and self-awareness. They continue to need form and structure in their physical environment, while still living in the world of the imagination. They gradually become more self-aware through observation of their surroundings as separate from themselves. The garden provides an opportunity to build a healthy understanding of the complex relationships of the plant and animal kingdoms.

The second grader is able to take up individual tasks. Their fine motor skills allow them to grasp seeds and plant them individually rather than casting them out as a group. Larger seeds—of pea, radish, corn, or sunflower—can be grasped and put in the earth with intention and care. Reflection on their behavior and the results of their actions becomes more conscious than in previous years.

Simple observations in the garden connect the children with their surroundings, as they begin noticing the habitats, nature, and unique qualities of animals. Why does the squirrel hide its nuts? How do birds behave differently in winter and spring? Why are the geese flying together? In striving to find the soul qualities and gestures behind the animals' behavior, the teacher brings an imaginative awareness to the student that gives meaning to these observations. At this age, finding commonalities between the human and animal kingdoms, which share an ability to sense their environment, allows us to find positive and negative aspects of the animal's behavior within ourselves.

Silent nature walks open children to their surroundings in a new way. Activities such as hearing the howling wind, seeing the summer breeze, or listening to bird calls, train the senses to perceive the natural world. Taking time to observe what is happening underground, by picking up logs or stones, can give the young child a sense for all the soil organisms they are naturally drawn to, such as worms, caterpillars, beetles, and centipedes. Children can be brought to notice a beginning bud as well as an open flower. This awareness builds the foundation for the sciences in later years.

Third Grade Consciousness

Before third grade, children are at one with their surroundings. Slowly the child begins to feel separate. This leads to new questions about their place in the world and is a step towards independence and objectivity. The transition is sometimes called the "nine-year-change," and can be a time of loneliness and uncertainty until the child reemerges sometime around nine-and-a-half to ten years old with a new sense of belonging, much like the chrysalis transforming into the butterfly.

For the first time the child begins to notice all that is done around them to sustain their life. They seek to understand their part in it all. They may lose some of the trust they have had that their needs will be provided for. They start to wonder how they would survive in the world if they had to be independent of their parents. At this time it is especially helpful to guide their attention to workers and tradespeople, who contribute to our survival. Within this world of practical, life sustaining activities, the farmer is central. The farmer's work is to grow the food that nourishes our bodies. Through the gardening class, third graders begin to see farmers and farming as a path to security. Engaging in the practical work of the farm helps children to trust their place in the world and provides ongoing lessons of gratitude and responsibility.

When the third grader is able to experience the whole process of how something is made, they feel more secure. Bread, the staff of life, is taken from seed to loaf through planting, cultivating, harvesting, winnowing, threshing, grinding, and baking. The understanding of where our bread comes from and our part in the process makes baking and eating bread a sacred act.

> The silver rain, the shining sun,
> The fields where scarlet poppies run,
> and all the ripples of the wheat,
> are in the bread that I do eat.
> So when I sit for every meal,
> with thankful heart I always feel,
> that I am eating rain and sun,
> and fields where scarlet poppies run.
> —Alice C. Henderson

To build a house, make clothes, spin wool, make butter and cheese, and grow grain gives the third grader confidence in their ability to make their way in the world.

Fourth Grade Consciousness

In fourth grade, the child's sense of self grows stronger, as does their strength of will.

Finding confidence in their place on the earth and in their bodies, they begin looking out into the world around them. Through practical work they must meet physical challenges and develop their forces of will. The fourth grader is now building on their imaginative thinking by developing observational thinking. This is supported through direct observation of the natural habitats of plants, animals, birds, and insects. Learning about local geography and how indigenous people lived on the land gives the child a sense of completeness—everything is right there to provide for our needs.

In the garden, this new-found sense of self can find expression in caring for the animals, cleaning cages and stalls, transporting manure from the animal housing to the compost pile. This service provided for the animals recognizes and respects the animal's gifts to us: eggs, milk, wool, and meat. Thoroughly getting to know, love, and understand an animal at this age can be a powerful and healing experience for the feeling life of a fourth grader. To accurately observe the animal, the way it stands, moves, eats, its color, shape, and more, helps the child see their own "animal-ness," and opens a more compassionate and caring side of themselves. They see the patience of the cow, the shyness of the sheep and the impulsiveness of the chicken.

Fifth Grade Consciousness

With the fifth grader's growing capacities and greater sense of self comes an ability to differentiate. While the pictorial imagination is still present, at this age the child can begin to formulate concepts. Their comprehension is increasing. In their classroom work in botany, the child can begin to see the details of life's interrelatedness. They learn to differentiate the plant parts, yet also bring the parts together into the whole and see the plant as part of a larger plant community.

In the classroom and the garden, the children follow the development of the plant from one stage to another, gaining an instinctive feeling for organic evolution as an example of striving toward perfection. When a child is given an objective picture of growth that parallels their own, something is strengthened in their own being. Uncertainties of life are overcome by learning that there is a pattern in the world that has a lawfulness and continuity. The growth of leaves at every node is an example of this lawfulness that we take for granted. The raspberry begins as a flower and turns into a red berry every time.

In order to build a relationship with plants and flowers, they spend time drawing, drying, pressing, and collecting them. By observing root development the child can notice how a plant connects to the earth. The poppy, with its many seeds, gives a picture of reproduction. Children notice the birds and insects living around them. They see the relationship between the butterfly and the flower when they see butterflies drawn to the echinacea. They watch the caterpillar transform into a butterfly. Questions and observations lead the student to a greater understanding of the natural world, and they see processes of growth that parallel their own development.

While students often prefer hands-on learning as a break from the routine of deskwork, many activities demand a deeper look at the lesson behind the experience through written work. Student journal-books can be an effective tool for written work, to help document weather observations, do plant drawings, or write poetry. These books are especially good for fifth and sixth grade students.

Sixth Grade Consciousness

In sixth grade, the authority of the adult is challenged by the child's new reasoning capacity. This pushing against the boundaries is a natural stage and will assure the child that there are still boundaries in place to hold them as they experience all of the many changes that puberty brings. Along with puberty comes the ability for logical and analytical thinking. The child can now connect cause and effect.

As they enter adolescence, they begin to experience a heaviness. The body, that was once "all head," has grown in muscle and bones. As gravity pulls on them, they must find their physical strength. Glands and sexual organs are maturing and the limbs are growing. The sinuous, fibrous tissues that connect muscles to bones are now developed and strong enough for the child to use proper farm tools. The hard work of double digging, building compost piles, and hauling and shoveling manure helps them to learn to direct their new physical capacities. The physical work arouses the young person's craving for knowing, and the intellectual work is furthered by physical work.

The student's physical bodies meet with resistance in hard work with the earth. This is a parallel picture of the resistance they meet with authority, peers, and their changing selves. There is a certain emotional weightiness that is served by the demands of hard work. The spade and digging fork are important tools. As they meet, penetrate, and cultivate the soil, they face themselves and their friends with a growing social awareness. Just as it is difficult to push the spade into the earth, they must push through social and emotional challenges.

Observational skills come into form with more structure and attention to detail. Flowers, through their scent, form, and color, are of particular interest since the adolescent has greater focus on personal likes and dislikes. They can begin to take their own initiative, but since the sense of self isn't fully in place the teacher's guidance is still necessary. At this age we strive to have the student persist through tasks without constant reminders, building the strength to be directed more readily by their own inner authority. The child seeks and meets resistance in order to further the growth of their self-directed will. They are becoming masters of the garden, and can share knowledge out of experience. This inner authority is a newly sprouting seed that needs great care in the coming years. An example of this is seen in the sixth grade knighting ceremony practiced in many Waldorf schools. The students choose a personal goal and service project for which they will be publicly recognized. This uprightness in their will gives direction to their judgment and keeps them striving to achieve their highest good.

Seventh Grade Consciousness

In seventh grade, the child has transitioned through the trials of sixth grade and begins to find respect and appreciation for their teachers again. Along with this comes a capacity for outer and inner reflection. There can be a tension between the child's budding sexual identity and a less-developed psychological maturity. In the garden we support the classroom lessons on anatomy and physiology by studying nourishment while bringing awareness to the systems of the body and how food choices support these systems. Healing plants, personal health, and hygiene all interest the student as they become more aware of their changing physical form. The study of health and nutrition in the lesson comes alive in cooking. The cultivation of vegetables for cooking, and flowers that feed the soul, give interest and purpose to one's work. Gaining knowledge of the outer world gives a sense of certainty for the developing inner world.

At this time a sense for aesthetics can be made manifest in the act of designing a garden plot and maintaining order. This outer sense of order and beauty can help to bring order to the inner life. As they strengthen their sense of self, the student becomes capable of the more demanding work of growing food for their community.

Farming classes in the seventh grade are a counter-balance to the tendency to go towards materialism and the lure of advertising, or the opposite—to withdraw and become isolated. The constancy of farming and the need for the students to apply themselves to the task can be the middle ground between withdrawal and self-centeredness.

Eighth Grade Consciousness

In grade eight, emancipation, independence, and individuation call for greater responsibility and differentiation. In the garden, logical thinking and free and independent judgment are encouraged. Smaller groups work over a period of time at more specialized tasks.

Their need for independence can be recognized and encouraged by giving them more responsibility, leadership, and choices. Students can achieve more at this age by the teacher holding high expectations without criticism. The self-absorption at this age is countered by service projects and working through one's resistance to challenges.

Ninth Grade Consciousness

In the high school, gardening can be done in blocks along with many different art and craft options, each calling for the development of different capacities. Tending the earth helps foster love by caring for all that lives around us, and unites the high school student with the ideas and ideals that they are unconsciously longing for. In grade nine, a strong wish to engage with life must find a place where these ideals are upheld and made manifest. The search for independence waxes and wanes and can create a roller coaster of emotions. The birthing of logical thinking can be lonesome, while social passions and desires pull at the student's sense of self.

In the garden, ninth grade is an apprenticeship year. To stand with the master and learn new skills and concepts gives a place for the student's newly forming capacities for logical thinking. The principles and practices of biodynamic agriculture and permaculture are introduced. The student's longing and love for the earth can be fully enjoyed in the care and maintenance of their garden plot. They have more responsibility for working independently, and now that they know how to handle tools, their work is more accurate. They take direction well and want to follow the master. They want to be a master themselves in order to gain the independence they seek at this age.

Tenth Grade Consciousness

Tenth grade is a time of polarities, an inward focus paired with a wish to find principles that are true in the outer world. Students see things in black and white—in extremes. It is normal at this age for the student to grow critical as they attempt to find the middle: their own center. To find the balance point between the polarities, the student must come to what is truthful. The curriculum can help them to live in the polarities as a way of learning, while not staying in the extremes. Students are encouraged to look into the world and find practical applications of knowledge put into service by human beings. Now they can see the farm as it relates to the community. Farm economics, along with seasonal and local food marketing, all must function in farming. These practices give the student tools to know that they can enhance their agricultural environment and make the world a better place.

Eleventh Grade Consciousness

In eleventh grade the light begins to shine. Interest in others and in world issues spurs social service projects and self-directed learning. They now have the skills and the stronger sense of self to take their work seriously and meet many of the environmental challenges with ideas and ideals that they have cultivated. At this age, their idealism must be kept buoyant. They can get despondent and overwhelmed if they dwell only on the problems. In both eleventh and twelfth grades, the teacher becomes a resource and the student becomes the leader.

Eleventh grade students are more analytical. Their questions are real and very specific. They want valid answers. This seeking is a strong force in giving intention to their work, as well as strengthening their belief that they have a place in the world and a skill that they can offer. They want solutions they can implement.

While students of this age are immersing themselves in technology and all it has to offer, the gardening curriculum can be an antidote to an unbalanced dependence. Delegating tasks and skills to a computer can be very useful but it robs us of the need to develop our own knowledge.

Eleventh and twelfth graders are encouraged to build on their formerly acquired gardening skills and capacities and invest themselves in gardening projects that they are personally interested in.

Twelfth Grade Consciousness

In twelfth grade, the gardening and farming curriculum culminates with students bringing their farming skills to those in need. Self-knowledge becomes rightful action, and student's benefit from a large amount of freedom. They take on and complete projects of their choice. The true individuality of the student is able to thrive in such an environment.

In twelfth grade the study of world ecology and the practices of biodynamic and permaculture gardening are deepened. The twelfth grader's stronger sense of self gives them the foundation upon which to explore and implement these complex agricultural methods. The question, "What is man's responsibility for the earth?" can be taken up individually and as a group. They understand that the earth is a living being and wish to find their role as stewards. The curriculum builds on itself throughout the years and comes to its completion with the twelfth grader finding the tools to meet the world of today.

3 Curriculum Development & Self-Development

As we meet and touch each day,
The many travelers on our way,
Let every brief contact be
A glorious helpful ministry.
The contact of the soil and seed

Each giving to the other's need
Each helping on the other's quest
And blessing each as well as blessed.

—*Susan Coolidge*

CHILDREN OF ALL AGES need structure, rhythm, and repetition. Structure provides security. Though the child may not be consciously aware of the form brought by the teacher, the child can sense and find security in the fact that the adult is in charge. The rhythm of the structure is reinforcing: what repeats itself becomes familiar and what is familiar creates security. A structure is built with repetition and the passage of time, and the building of it begins the moment a teacher first has contact with the students. A formal greeting is always a good beginning:

"Good morning, Class Three."

"Good morning, Ms. Sands."

A formal greeting helps children and youth of all ages know that the lesson has begun and now the teacher is in charge—it is time to look and listen.

Often the class begins outside, so form in space is also important. Meet and greet the children at the same place. This helps students to build a relationship to the start of the lesson. What happened before will happen again. On some level, students become secure in the "sameness" and can relax and receive what is being taught.

In Waldorf education there is an emphasis on storytelling as a tool for developing the child's imagination. This prepares the child for abstract thinking, which comes in later lessons. Abstraction without the foundation of imaginative picturing limits the capacity to be a creative thinker. Imaginative pictures are alive and these pictures can be added to and grow with the child's understanding and development throughout the years in the garden.

At Summerfield Waldorf School we begin and end each lesson for the younger children under an old walnut tree. To one side there is a circle of picnic tables where the students sit on the outside benches facing the tree. I stand in front of the tree. Once we greet each other, the students sit down and I tell a story that gives the imaginative picture of the lesson. "The Little Red Hen," for example, is such a perfect story for the planting of wheat and it carries a hidden moral lesson as well.

In gardening, this capacity to imagine that comes with listening to stories, helps a child work with the unseen forces of nature. The growing seed, the warming sun, the deep, dark roots, are all full of life and change over time. Many processes are unseen or meaningless without our ability to imagine and picture the part of the process that happens underground or at night or too slowly for our senses to perceive.

In Waldorf Education teachers memorize the story and tell it to the children from the pictures that we see in our own imagination. What we see in our imagination makes it possible for the child to create those pictures in her imagination as well. Reading from the page introduces a level of abstraction that breaks the picture imagining that puts the teller and the listener directly in the story. Memorize a story by taking it in parts. Get a feel for the sounds of certain words or phrases and then picture every part. For example, with "The Little Red Hen," as the teacher practices the words, "The dog liked to sleep on the sunny back porch. The cat would rest in the old chair by the fireplace," the teacher is picturing vividly what they are describing and are thereby able to remember it exactly. It is a powerful process to look at the children while telling a story and to see their wide eyes and faces soothed by the ability to rest in their imagination.

A story can also be "made up"—a tale of how the farmer found the corn seed, or what the cow ate for lunch. As long as the story represents truth and is not arbitrary fantasy, it can be healthy to bring ideas you wish to share with the children in the less didactic form of a "story." Starting in the fourth grade it is appropriate to make up your own story based on the lesson of the day. For example, if we are mucking out the sheep's pen, you might start out by asking the students, "What is it like when you have wet shoes and socks for a long time? Well, the sheep are standing in cold, wet straw and they would really like to have it removed and replaced with fresh, dry straw." The story goes on from there and leads us to the task for the day.

Once the story is told, it is time to get to work. Start with a very clear description of the activities, and break the children up into groups of seven to ten children. The gardening teacher supervises these groups with an assistant teacher, the class teacher, or volunteers so that the students have more room to work and enough supervision. More detailed instructions are given to each group. With the planting of wheat, for example, the first group will fill the flats with soil, the second group will plant the wheat, and the third group will prepare the bed where the wheat will be planted. It will take four weeks before the wheat is ready to go into the bed. At the end of the lesson students and teacher gather and reflect on the work done. For example, the teacher may speak about the wheat seeds in their flats, waiting for Father Sun to warm the soil so the green sprouts can emerge.

Steps to Prepare a Lesson

1. Rhythm in the lesson (in-breath and out-breath): "In-breaths" include welcome and greeting at the beginning, gathering for a snack, and gathering to reflect on the session and to say goodbye at the end. "Out-breaths" take place as children do physical work and engage in activities. Some concentrated work, like sowing seeds, can be more of an "in-breath." A strong opening "in-breath" makes it possible to let the students "breathe out" during the work time, as long as the "out-breath" is intentional. If rascally behavior shows up, the teacher can help the student to relocate their intention and bring it back to their work ("breathe-in").

Sometimes this might mean changing the work task to one that brings them "in." For a sixth grader, splitting wood can help bring them in. If you are experiencing challenges, you may need to question whether you are really allowing the children to go "out" or if there is too much control. This could also be a reflection of their other classes, if there has been an imbalance of concentrated work. The "out-breath" works best when it is two to three times as long as the "in-breath," and even longer still with adolescents and high school students.

2. Memorize the story: this takes time and practice. The best advice for this task is to inwardly see everything that happens in the story, and to tell the story from what you see. Always use the same words, the same sequence, so you can stay in your imagination. This way, you only have to tell it, not think it through. Another aid in memorization is to walk or pace while practicing. If you engage your will forces at the same time that your imagination is bringing feeling to the story, and your mind is grasping the order of events, you are applying your willing, feeling, and thinking.

3. Have all the supplies prepared, ready, and on hand. For example, a jar of seeds, a wheelbarrow of soil, flats for receiving soil, watering cans, a place ready in the greenhouse, etc. As the children get older, in some cases, gathering materials together can become a work task for them.

4. Give a brief overview of the activities of the day to assistant teachers, class teachers, and/or volunteers, and be clear what you are asking of them. Be clear that they should guide the children rather than doing the work themselves.

5. Some lessons lend themselves to songs or movement games, and these all must be prepared and memorized ahead of time. Movement and singing help harmonize the group and prepare the children for what is to come. This comes after the story or can take the place of a story.

6. There are many spontaneous lessons that occur in the moment and we must be ready for these. For example, when I saw that we had a sunflower with an

enormous seed head, I thought we should save the seeds. I found a gold mesh bag and told the children that we needed a queen who would receive a crown and we must find the sunflower that most deserved the golden crown. When we all agreed on who she would be, we placed the crown upon her head (the mesh bag) and now her special seeds would be saved in the bag for all generations to come. The simplest of stories can have the deepest meaning.

7. Evaluate and adjust your lesson: This can happen during a lesson or upon reflection. Take notes, notice if the groups were well balanced, if the activity was a good fit, and whether the tasks were completed or not.

8. Lessons and activities can be brought back throughout the grades, each time at a deeper level.

Long-Range Lesson Planning

Lesson planning can be approached in a number of different ways:

1. Nature is an overriding factor in curriculum development. Walk through the garden on a regular basis with a clipboard and note what you see and what needs attention. Then imagine the classes that will be coming that week, noting which activities are appropriate for each grade.

2. Look at the year, break it up into months and look at seasonal activities. Again, look at which grades will be there on which days and make your plan accordingly. (See grade specific chapters for activity ideas).

3. Take the activity—say plant propagation—and knowing that this is being taught to an eleventh grade class, list all of the different methods, definitions, and explanations you may want to use. Use a chalkboard to illustrate these: for example seeding, division, layering, and cuttings. Then break the students up into three or four groups. One group makes the seeding mix, another does seed saving, another group can propagate by cuttings, while others propagate strawberries by layering.

4. Respond to conditions in the moment: If cases of apples are donated, or all of

the basil is about to bolt, or if all the tomatoes are ripe, the lesson becomes making apple sauce, blending and freezing pesto, or roasting and freezing tomatoes. Flexibility is a necessity in garden teaching. You still have to think through all of the steps, all of the equipment needed, where the activity will take place, and even have all of your freezer bags ready. Because gardening it is a living, ever-changing curriculum, you must work with what is happening in nature.

Classroom Management

Here are some ingredients for a healthy relationship with your students and a healthy class dynamic:

1. Cultivate and model the qualities of warmth, interest, and respect towards the students.
2. Create a listening space that comes to silence, especially when opening and closing the lesson. (This is a space where only one person speaks and everyone else listens. I call on students who raise their hands. I speak only when everyone is quiet.)
3. Build good work habits by repeating and demonstrating how a tool is used and what your goals are for using a particular tool.
4. Encourage problem solving, especially with older children. With younger children problems are solved with positive examples rather than direct questions to the student. Starting in fourth and fifth grade, and especially by high school, challenge them with questions before you give all of the answers. This can be done in the smaller groups so students are not on the spot with the entire class.
5. Create a balance between social interactions and working independently.
6. Keep an awareness of the four temperaments as well as individual learning styles or modalities. Give children tasks that meet them in a way that allows them to be successful as well as appropriately challenged. Address individual differences with pedagogically appropriate projects. For example, Lucy is a very strong, energetic

girl going into fifth grade. Rather than ask her to gather seed heads for seed sav-ing, ask her to haul a cartload of weeds and feed them to the chickens. While it might challenge her in a good way to gather seed heads, it doesn't make use of her natural strengths. Giving her something that allows her strength to be utilized gives her more confidence in herself.

7. The length of time of gardening classes is important to establishing a healthy rhythm. Simple activities for kindergarten through second grade can easily be ac-commodated in a forty-five minute to one hour session. Third grade through high school classes require one-and-a-half hours, although many lessons may have to fit into fifty-five minute slots.

8. Keep transitions in mind: plan how you move from the introduction, to the tool, to the work, to the clean up. The end of the lesson, which is just as important as the beginning, can include collecting tools, cleaning them, counting to make sure all the tools are back from the garden, and closing the lesson with a reflection and a good-bye. Because it's a living lesson, it is hard sometimes to calculate the time; you have to be flexible and adapt to the reality of what happens. With older chil-dren, tool cleanup can become the closing along with a goodbye and thank you. With younger children, however, a structured closing should not be sacrificed.

9. Keep a record of each child's developing capacities and skills. This is best done daily, at the end of the workday. Reflect on the quality of the work, self-motiva-tion, respectfulness, engagement, struggles, and obstacles to overcome. This leads to a question of the meditative or reflective role of the teacher, which is addressed later on.

10. Keep a record of the lesson itself; what worked and what didn't.

Classroom management is very different in an outdoor setting. First of all, there are no walls or desks, the children are in movement, and they may be using tools. Walls, desks, and chairs help the students find their secure place in the classroom and allow the classroom teacher to work with individual students while others are occupied with their work. The ratio of teacher to student needs to be greater in an outdoor space, and it may fall on the gardening teacher, as the specialist, to educate her colleagues on this matter. The help of a classroom teacher, an assistant, parent volunteers, or rotating half or a third of the class are all possible solutions to making a class manageable.

Secondly, some children confuse gardening class with recess and need help seeing the difference. Bringing children into form and reverence with their work takes time and good modeling. A teacher must be able to see everyone at all times, while not loosing the big picture. A well-planned lesson, and one that meets them developmentally, stimulates the interest and engagement of the students and is the strongest fabric to hold their attention.

Another key element is the relationship between the teacher and student. Students have a strong sense for being "seen" by the teacher. A teacher who can acknowledge each student, even once a week, can build this relationship over time and become a guide rather than a policeman. Practically speaking, taking notes on each child will help you to succeed in connecting with them.

As the teacher breathes, so does the student. Another tool in classroom management is to literally breathe deeply throughout the lesson. "Breathing" in the emotional realm, is important: show joyfulness and humor, yet be clear and strong in your expectations of the students. If you show excitement and interest in what the children are going to be working on in the garden they will want to participate and take up the work. To those more used to working with adolescents or adults, or for new teachers, this enthusiasm can seem put-on at first, since we often loose this simple enthusiasm as we age, but with practice it will feel more natural.

The most important tool for discipline is to build positive experiences with each individual child. These positive experiences form a healthy ground from which to address any behavior problems that may crop up from time to time. If you notice that discipline issues are coming up with a child, a great practice is, over time, to intentionally find ways to have positive interactions, no matter how small, as you also directly address the behavioral issue.

Objectivity is the best practice for addressing specific behaviors. Speak to a child directly, then ask what happened or what they were trying to do. Then tell her what you saw, and what is appropriate and not appropriate. You can sometimes ask them if they understand what you mean, and if they are willing to change. For example: "I see your hoe going up in the air. Were you doing that to get the work done faster? Hoes work best when they come up only this far off the ground. Let me show you. See how this works? Let me see you try it this way." This objectivity helps to separate the behavior or action from the intrinsic being of the child. Asking the child what they were trying or intending to do gives them the opportunity to explain a possibly good motive that was simply paired with an unskillful method, and again helps them to feel seen and cared for by the teacher. What is of utmost importance is to avoid punishing, shaming, or shunning children as this can cause damage to the child.

Weather can often be a challenge in classroom management and a garden teacher must work with the classroom teacher to make sure that the students come to class appropriately dressed. Sun hats and water bottles are very helpful in the hot weather, while boots and rain gear make it possible to still have a lesson in the rain. In the autumn, winter, and early spring, plan for an indoor as well as outdoor lesson, just in case the rain becomes too heavy. Chaos can easily develop in the rain, so a tighter lesson plan is needed.

In an outdoor setting, safety must be a first concern. Set clear rules and boundaries from the beginning. A few examples include:

- No running
- No throwing
- Ask before picking
- Respect all creatures, plants, and tools

Proper tool use will be an ongoing safety concern, and keeping students a certain distance from each other takes diligence and keen eyes. An atmosphere of reverence and respect must be continually reinforced. For example, with the young child, showing them the relationship between their hand and the shape of a trowel, can be a place to model gratitude that we can use a tool in place of our hand. Tools go to those who truly honor them because of the service that they do for us. If a tool is being misused or damaged, proper use would be modeled again, and the teacher would ask the question of whether they are really ready to use the tool. The capacity to perfect their love and appreciation for tools comes with work well done.

Collegial Relationships & School Community

Collegial relationships are essential and the door swings both ways. Teachers may ask to cut flowers for a bouquet or have a writing lesson in the garden, while the nursery class wants to visit the garden to pick grapes.

Welcoming others at times when there are no classes in the garden builds community and helps everyone to feel interested and connected to the ongoing changes and evolution in the garden. Festivals and school events are another way to integrate the gardening program and to build collegial relationships. On a back-to-school workday parents and students can help with weeding and pruning after a summer of rampant growth. Class fundraisers can also have a garden component: canning salsa from garden tomatoes, or baking pumpkin muffins. Or have a third grade Thanksgiving Feast and invite all the parents. Other examples of collegial collaboration include: working with the fourth grade class teacher to raise fish as a study of watersheds; creating craft projects from the garden as a holiday gift; carving pumpkins for Halloween; or canning or baking for a class fundraiser. The opportunities are endless, but your energy is not. There are boundaries and times to say no. If there is a class in the garden, it is not a good time for a high school science class to come for a visit.

As a gardening teacher, especially if part-time, it is sometimes hard to find where to fit into the faculty structure. At Summerfield, in the high school, gardening is considered an art class that fits into the art rotation. There the gardening instructor teaches other subjects, and attends all meetings. This helps to create a sense of being part of the larger school community and allows the gardening instructor to stay connected with the ongoing updates on students and school issues. Becoming a salaried faculty member with additional funded roles can help the gardening teacher to be seen and appreciated among the faculty. This could include coordinating a summer camp program, overseeing students' community service, being a class advisor, or other needed roles in the school.

Another route to becoming a full faculty member is to create an expanded or even all-day gardening/outdoor education/practical activities program. Such programs are increasingly needed as children with challenges in the classroom setting often learn and thrive when academics are blended with practical activities.

Whichever route you take, getting a seat on the faculty will ensure the gardening program's long-term viability in the school and protects teachers from the "burnout" that can result from a lack of sufficient support. If the gardening teacher is not able to become a faculty member, it helps to bring in an outside consultant who can objectively present the necessity for the skills gardening teaches. Being able to communicate the relationships between garden work and academics is necessary to justify a program to administrators and parents. An expert in outdoor education can lend credibility to what is already known about gardening/outdoor education programs: that eco-literacy, ecology, and sustainability studies are essential to healthy development and can lead to careers in sustainable fields.

If the gardening teacher position cannot be full time, the role can easily remain misunderstood and underappreciated. A curriculum that works with living beings and is dependent on a person to care for those living beings has very different time and supply requirements than other specialty subject curriculums. As they fill out the "specialties" schedule, administrators or other faculty simply may not recognize that a gardening teacher needs paid preparation and work hours in the garden. It is very important to put in writing a program description and budget including the necessary time and materials. It helps to find at least one other person in the school to help you brainstorm and advocate for items that the program might need.

Self-Development

My own love and care for the earth has a role in developing my work with the children. I am continually asking myself the question, "What is my task in redeeming nature and caring for the earth and how does my work with the children in the garden serve this task at this time?" As a teacher it is important to keep a broader vision in mind while tending the details of the day. This vision imbues my work with the spiritual foundations behind Waldorf education.

The whole developmental process from birth to twenty-one is a process of incarnation; of the physical, etheric, emotional, and ego bodies being gradually penetrated with capacities and awareness by the spiritual being of the child. This incarnation process happens at different rates for different children. Sensory integration is the capacity to balance the senses, and have a clear path for the sensory input to travel to other parts of the body and brain. Movement is vital for healthy sensory integration.

Observe the children at work. This reveals a lot about the elements that the student is composed of, and what their strengths and weaknesses are. For instance, how they use a tool can show how incarnated they are into their physical body. This observation leads to insights into what activities could best serve their development.

Many great ideas can be gleaned from the quiet, reflective time that a teacher spends looking back on the day. What worked, what didn't? How did the activity meet the students? Were there any students who were challenging, needy, leaders, successfully meeting a challenging task? What excited them? When were they inspired? How were they engaged? Strive to teach toward the child's "higher self," that part of the student who is the all-knowing self. The child does not have this in place yet, it is just in seed form, but it is reachable and teachable and can bring insights. Let the student know you see their positive attributes and capacities, even when they're not showing them, so that they can realign themselves with something better. Give them an option to change their ways without being critical. In addition, the acts of observation and meditation can affect change. Positive change can happen simply because on some level a child knows when you acknowledge their "higher self."

Insights gleaned during observation and meditation can be fodder for how you plan future lessons and how you meet the students differently, or pay more attention to someone, give a leadership role, or even have a further conversation with the class teacher. Reflection is a rich resource that pulls up the awareness that isn't noticed in the busy moment. These insights can, of course, also come during a lesson in the form of an insight that a child or a class would be helped by a particular activity. Being open to such guidance can lead to just the right thing at the right time, but does not replace careful planning.

Keeping inspired, alive, and awake is an ongoing process. A teacher is supported by a rhythmical life. Plan less and rest more, and the answers will come. A teacher who is working outside and is physically engaged most of the day must take time to replenish their energy.

Reading the weekly verses in Rudolf Steiner's *Calendar of the Soul* gives one a picture of the seasonal relationship between the human being, the earth, and the cosmos. This reinforces the right attitude and mood to bring to our teaching at a given time of the year. It also helps to build one's inner life, which is an important component in Waldorf Education. Our "higher self" needs cultivating through study, practice, and meditation, in order that we might become more aware of the spiritual behind the physical in our students, as well as the "Spiritual Being of Nature." The *Calendar of the Soul* is helpful in guiding one to see and experience the spiritual relationship between self and nature, and between the cosmic and the earthly forces at work in the garden. Here's an example for Autumn (Week 30):

> *In sunlight of my soul are sprouting now*
> *The ripening fruits of thinking;*
> *To certainty of conscious self*
> *All feeling now transforms itself.*
> *Now I can sense in joyful mood*
> *The autumn spirit waking:*
> *The winter will in me*
> *Wake the summer of the soul.*
> *—Rudolf Steiner (trans. D. Aldan)*

As I reflect on this verse I see the three seasons that are mentioned and see how I am weaving my sense of self into the fabric of nature's seasonal changes. How is my soul a reflection of these transitions?

Meditation helps us to sensitize ourselves to what is around us and be able to respond with consciousness and wisdom. Rudolf Steiner says that the pace of our breathing is slightly changed during meditation, which brings us to a different experience of the world around us. This sensitivity leads to insights that give guidance and inspiration, helping our work with the children to become a reflection of this insight.*

Maintaining & Developing the Gardening Craft

Being a good gardening teacher means keeping your craft and skills up to date. It is interesting that the teacher for the most part is not the doer, but the conductor of an orchestra. The necessary gardening and farming skills must be practiced when the children are not there. Skill with tools and knowledge of plants lives in the limbs and is reawakened during work. Allow time to keep in practice by working when the children are not there. This work reminds us of why we love to garden and how joyful it can be. Learn from every weed you pull and every plant you prune.

---

* See *Agriculture*, Rudolf Steiner, Chapter 3, p. 55 (The Biodynamic Farming & Gardening Association, Kimberton, PA 1993).

One way of deepening the craft is to join a biodynamic study group. In the winter weeks, the Agriculture lectures given by Rudolf Steiner in 1924 are read and discussed, taking one lecture per week. Meeting with other garden teachers on a regular basis to share curriculum ideas and garden questions is helpful.

Visiting other farms and gardens is very inspiring and gives a new look at someone else's ideas that can awaken new possibilities. Workshops are also a good way to awaken questions and ideas and to have conversations with teachers and other people who are practicing farming and gardening in a variety of settings.

4   Biodynamic Agriculture Demystified

The understanding that Mother Nature is now ailing and that Humanity must take the responsibility to nurture our Mother back to health is inherent in the Biodynamic approach. It is this responsibility to the earth and this healing, holistic approach which can bring to education what is most especially needed in our age.
—*Perry Hart, Founding Farmer, Summerfield Waldorf School and Farm*

FROM A NUTRITIONAL VIEWPOINT, we gain physical vitality from food only when we are able to fully break it down through our digestion. The more vital our food is, the more vitality we receive from it. The vitality in food can be called "life forces." Growing food biodynamically means that we are not merely concerned with the appearance of the food, but are concerned with growing food that has an abundance of "life forces" as well as mineral nutrients. In order to grow healthy, vital plants, the soil must be rich with life.

We enliven soil and build up organic matter by composting a variety of materials: vegetable waste, manure, leaves, food scraps, etc. All contain precious nutrients, and feed biological life. The compost pile can be seen as the digestive organ of the farm itself. Soil enriched and enlivened in this way is said to be rich in organic matter, thus the name "organic." In biodynamic agriculture we strive to continually enlist the help of living organisms in order to grow healthy food. A dynamic "force" is one that motivates and effects development. Plants grow best in soil that releases nutrients in a continuous way. Because the biodynamic farmer has given the soil adequate materials and forces, it will have the highest amount of nutrients and energy available to the plants and then to the person who is eating the food.

Farmers in the early 1900s already saw that the productivity and health of crops were decreasing. Rudolf Steiner told farmers that the biodynamic preparations (remedies for depleted soil) would help make valuable trace minerals available to the plants through the soil, thereby improving human nutrition, but in a much broader sense than is commonly held. The biodynamic compost preparations are similar to a cell phone tower broadcasting information. They "radiate" and attract certain life forces that can teach the plants grown in the resulting compost to find the micro and macronutrients they need. When asked by one of his students why people were not able to carry out their spiritual intentions more easily, Steiner replied, "This is a problem of nutrition. Nutrition as it is today does not supply the strength necessary for manifesting the spirit in physical life. A bridge can no longer be built from thinking to will and action. Food plants no longer contain the forces people need for this."* Biodynamic farmers strive to reduce harm, heal the earth, and provide people with the vitality they need to carry out their life goals and purposes with strong will forces.

Rudolf Steiner's Spiritual Science

Rudolf Steiner was born in Austria 1861 and died in 1925. He was a social scientist, philosopher, clairvoyant, and artist. He began his career as a spiritual teacher as the head of the German branch of the Theosophical Society and later founded his own group, the Anthroposophical Society (*Anthropo*—human; *Sophia*—wisdom). Though he was born with a certain ability to see realms of existence that our normal senses cannot perceive (clairvoyance), he further developed his capacities through meditation and spiritual practices meant to bring objectivity into spiritual perception. Throughout his life he developed his own perception to be able to see into suprasensible realms of reality. His task was to bring ancient truths into a language modern people could accept and embrace, and to create a new teaching appropriate to the

---

* Steiner as quoted by Ehrenfried Pfeiffer in his article "New Directions in Agriculture," in *Agriculture*, Bio-Dynamic Farming and Gardening Association, Kimberton, PA, 1993

current stage of human evolution and development. In spite of his vision into objective levels of suprasensible reality, typically he did not share his perceptions with others unless asked. This is one reason why he did not share information on the subject of agricultural until the end of his life.

Steiner began his 1924 lecture series by introducing his agricultural principals with an analogy. In his introductory remarks, he asked his listeners, would it be reasonable to think that a compass needle points north due solely to the materials from which it is made? Of course we know, and his listeners knew, that the compass needle is made of materials that *respond* to an invisible force—the magnetism of the earth itself. He then led his listeners to consider the many natural phenomena that contemporary science explains in a similar manner to claiming that the compass points north of its own volition. Contemporary science, he claimed, only describes half of the picture, the half that is dead material, and often ignores a whole set of forces that act on nature invisibly, yet do indeed exist—forces emanating from what he called the spiritual world.

Life itself is one such misunderstood phenomenon. Indeed, up until today, you would be hard pressed to find any scientific explanation of *life*, the force that vivifies living beings, other than electrical impulses. Yet, if electrical impulses were the cause of life, Mary Shelley's *Frankenstein* would have been a reality over a century ago. In 1901, when Dr. Duncan MacDougall attempted to isolate the life force by weighing bodies just prior to and just after death, his contemporaries at least found his question to be a valid one, while not agreeing with his methods or findings. Currently, over one hundred years later, contemporary scientists no longer consider finding the cause of life to be a scientifically worthwhile pursuit (especially if that cause could be outside of our sense perceptible world). There is simply silence. Yet life is there.

In Steiner's worldview, modern science by itself is dead science. In the moment that materials are dissected, or a natural process is recorded, it is no longer living, so the scientist cannot truly witness the forces and processes at work. His assertion that scientific thinking cannot, by definition, perceive unseen forces affecting our physical world has far reaching implications for people interested in finding a true science of agriculture. Is calcium simply calcium? Or might minerals transform depending on the life processes going on around them? In this way, the old ideas of alchemy become comprehensible.

With his compass analogy, Steiner in no way negated the importance of material science, but urged his listeners to marry it with its missing half—what he termed Spiritual Science. Steiner's "spiritual world," rather than being an abstract conception of a place elsewhere, such as heaven, is a series of interpenetrating "levels of being," some of which ordinary human senses and scientific instruments will never be able to measure. According to Steiner, the correct scientific instrument for perceiving these levels of being is our own spiritual perception, which any person can develop if they take the time and effort. In spiritual science the practitioner becomes one of the scientific instruments: through self-development exercises, one is slowly able to awaken a capacity to perceive spiritual forces and beings.

Steiner's cosmology, which describes our current historical moment in the context of vast time periods and a gradual evolution of consciousness, is central to understanding his biodynamic agriculture principals. In distant eras, all people were able to directly perceive something of the spiritual world, but they lacked individuality, free will, and a strong connection to the material world. He described how ancients retained the ability to perceive these levels of being, calling them, for instance in western culture, angelic realms. Steiner believed that collectively, over vast periods of time, we gradually lost our ability to perceive the suprasensible aspects of reality as we descended towards the farthest extreme of materialism, and physical matter was all that we could perceive or believe in. "For in the process of development, qualities of one kind passed over gradually into others; but before that time the last vestiges of ancient clairvoyance were still present... We can say that the development then begins of those faculties of soul which on the one hand confine [man's] power of judgment to the sense-perceptible world, while, on the other, they promote his self-consciousness."* That point was reached at the end of the nineteenth century and, according to Steiner, we are now beginning the long journey back to a full reunion with the beings and realities of the spiritual world, now with a developed individuality and free will. In order to achieve this, our current materialistic science will need to grow to encompass spiritual science.

In 1924, Steiner held a conference in Koberwitz, then part of Germany and now in Poland, which was attended by several hundred farmers, where he gave a series of eight lectures that form the basis of his biodynamic farming ideas. The study of these eight lectures provide a basis for farmers to implement Rudolf Steiner's ideas for agricultural renewal.

What differentiates biodynamic agriculture from conventional and organic agriculture are the following:

- The Earth is seen as an actual living being whose health is declining. The biodynamic farmer's task is to give the soil remedies to heal its continual depletion and, of course, to harm her as little as possible. Steiner gave instructions for making biodynamic "preparations" that would enhance soil intelligence and fertility. These preparations have biological ("*bio-*") aspects consisting of matter (various herbs and minerals), and "dynamic" aspects (consisting of life forces). Steiner described an Earth in decline, and urged that, "the benefits of the biodynamic preparations should be made available as quickly as possible to the largest possible areas of the entire Earth, for the Earth's healing."† If, as farmers, we did not continually take from the earth by cropping the same land over and over, these practices might not be as necessary. Since we do take and take, we must give back to help the Earth maintain homeostasis

---

* Steiner, Rudolf. *The Reappearance of Christ in the Etheric.* Lecture of March 6, 1910.
† Steiner as quoted by Ehrenfried Pfeiffer in his article "New Directions in Agriculture," in *Agriculture,* Bio-Dynamic Farming and Gardening Association, Kimberton, PA 1993

- Flowing from the reality that the Earth is a living being, each individual farm or garden is seen as a self-contained living organism. Sourcing your farm or garden inputs (such as nutrients, animal feed and seeds), to the greatest degree possible, from within this organism, supports its health and develops its individuality
- Plant nutrients are alive when they are delivered through the application of compost, biodynamic preparations and teas. In contrast, nutrients in chemical solution (powdered NPK fertilizers) that are used by conventional and some organic farmers and gardeners are dead—devoid of the life energy necessary to grow food with the proper nutrition for healthy human development
- All life on Earth is affected by the cosmos—the sun, moon and other planets in our solar system. The biodynamic farmer takes the cosmic rhythms and cycles into account in gardening activities in order to support a healthy farm organism and healthy crops. Biodynamic planting calendars that indicate celestial influences are available*

Biodynamic agriculture is a living process. While working to develop spiritual cognition, biodynamic farmers follow the indications and methods given by Steiner. Many of Steiner's students have developed spiritual cognition themselves and have been able to add new methods and refinements to the practice of biodynamic agriculture.

The Nine Biodynamic Preparations

The biodynamic farmer works to enhance the natural harmony of the whole farm organism through the use of compost, companion planting, cover cropping and the application of biodynamic preparations, which include herbs, minerals, and manures imbued by natural processes with life-enhancing qualities.

---

* Because of the precession of the equinox (gradual change in the earth's position relative to the stars of the galaxy), BD Farmers follow the actual celestial cycles (sidereal positions) as opposed to the celestial cycles followed by traditional western astrology, which don't take the precession of the equinox into account.

Almost all of the preparations that Steiner suggested are made up of herbs and many of them are aged in animal organs. Why animal organs? The organs, such as a stag bladder, or cow mesentery (the part of the cow intestine that transports the energy derived from food in the intestine to the liver), have a capacity to focus the power of formative forces streaming from the cosmos, transforming and enlivening the substances placed within them and eventually bringing these forces to the plants grown on the farm. Each organ has a relationship to a particular planet that endows it with spiritual forces; these forces act on the herbs within the organs. The preparations are buried beneath the ground ,where cosmic forces are more active, and are later dug up and diluted in water and sprayed on the land, or placed in the compost pile.

There are nine biodynamic preparations:

1. BD 500—*Horn Manure*   4. BD 503—*Chamomile*   7. BD 506—*Dandelion*
2. BD 501—*Horn Silica*   5. BD 504—*Stinging Nettle*   8. BD 507—*Valerian*
3. BD 502—*Yarrow*   6. BD 505—*Oak Bark*   9. BD 508—*Horsetail*

These can be grouped into two categories:

FIELD SPRAYS:

- BD 500—Horn Manure: Fresh cow manure that is packed into a cow horn and buried in the earth between spring and fall. After digging up, a small amount is diluted, rhythmically stirred in water, and sprayed on the soil before planting in order to enhance root development. This preparation is sprayed on the land at dusk.
- BD 501—Horn Silica: In spring, amethyst crystals or other silica rich crystals are ground down into a powder, packed in a cow horn and buried in the earth until fall. After aging, a very small amount is stirred rhythmically into water and sprayed on leafing, flowering, and fruiting crops in order to enhance flowering and fruiting. This preparation is sprayed at dawn.
- BD 508—Equisetum (horsetail) Tea: The horsetail plant, which itself is also very

high in silica, is steeped in rainwater to make a strong tea. If it's fermented fresh, it is steeped for two weeks. If made from the dried plant, it is simmered at a rate of four ounces of dried herb per gallon of water for thirty minutes. This is then diluted and sprayed on crops to enhance growth and prevent fungus and rot (Steiner emphasized that Equisetum spray was especially important to use in the Western hemisphere).

PREPARATIONS WHICH HAVE BEEN PROPERLY AGED AND THEN INSERTED INTO A NEWLY BUILT COMPOST PILE AND ALLOWED TO TRANSFORM ALONG WITH THE PILE:

- BD 502—Yarrow: Fresh or dried flowers are stuffed into a stag or elk bladder, hung in the sun during the summer and then buried in the earth for the winter.
- BD 503—Chamomile: Gathered in late spring, fresh or dried flowers are stuffed in a cow intestine and once dried are buried in the earth for the for the fall and winter.
- BD 504—Stinging Nettle: Cut in the Spring at the first flowering stage and buried in the earth in layers of screen or terra cotta pots and aged through the winter.
- BD 505—Oak Bark: Scraped from the tree mid-August to September, ground and stuffed into a cow or sheep skull; aged in a barrel under a water spout or a small stream through winter.
- BD 506—Dandelion: Gathered in Spring, fresh or dried blossoms are stuffed into a cow mesentery and aged in the ground through winter.
- BD 507—Valerian: In June fresh flowers are ground and pressed to extract the juice which is fermented for a few days in a glass bottle and then refrigerated or kept in a cool, dark place until use (sources disagree as to whether Steiner intended for BD 507 to be sprayed onto the compost pile when it is initially formed or just prior to use in the field).

Further study and practice of biodynamic methods is recommended in order to grasp the meaning behind the use of the preparations and their enhancement of the crops. Some of the polarities that help deepen these practices are cosmic vs. earthly forces; calcium vs. silica; and inner planets vs. outer planets. An in-depth study of

Rudolf Steiner's *Agriculture Course* is essential. A good "beginner's" text is *Culture and Horticulture* by Wolf D. Storl (see Bibliography).

Using the Biodynamic Preparations with Children

Using the biodynamic preparations with children and young people in the garden is a very open and variable question. It cannot really be prescribed or relegated to a particular grade or age. Become familiar with using the preparations yourself first and then decide what fits best for your situation.

Younger children can easily use a pine branch and bless a small section of the garden with the Horn Manure Preparation or the Equisetum Preparation in the spring. If you know a biodynamic farmer in your area, you could ask if they are making the preparations. Classes of younger students can gather dandelion blossoms, yarrow or chamomile, or, with gloves, stinging nettle as a gift for the farmer.

At Summerfield Waldorf School, the third graders apply a tree paste that contains horn manure and clay, which they paint on the apple trees in the spring. We speak about how the "magic mud" (horn manure) provides nutrients that the trees can take up through their bark and at the same time protects them from the elements. It provides food and medicine for the tree.

Sixth graders can collect fresh cow-dung for stuffing in horns to make the horn manure preparation. First, the students learn to differentiate between fresh and dried cow-pies. Wooden spoons or tongue depressors are used to push the manure tightly into the cow horns. The students learn that this will become a homeopathic medicine for the planting beds and in order for the cow-dung to turn to compost over winter it needs the protection of a vessel containing calcium—hence the cow horn. Seventh graders can treat seed potatoes with horn manure, ash, and chamomile tea as a protection against rot and enhancer of growth. Ninth graders can insert the compost preparations into finished piles. We talk about each herb bringing a unique quality to the pile, which will later be taken up by the plants that grow with the benefit of this compost.

High school students are certainly able to take up the ideas and the practice of biodynamic agriculture. When introducing biodynamic agriculture, start with the picture of the soil as an ecosystem, which feeds plants. We look at the life of the soil and its organic matter as well as the organisms and microorganisms within it. This is the storehouse of nutrients from which plants grow and these nutrients are then passed on to us when we consume the plants. Plants today give us less and less nutrition if soil is not vital (full of formative forces) and if the plants are not able to find a rich list of micronutrients. The preparations are homeopathic medicine made from herbs with specific qualities that will enhance the compost, which will then bring those qualities to the soil and the plants. The biodynamic preparations help vitalize the soil in a way that enhances nutritional value in the plants. In class we talk about each of the compost preparations, how they are made and what they bring to the soil via the compost. To touch, feel and see these preparations in action makes it real for the students.

Practical aspects include stirring and spraying Horn Manure and adding the preparations to compost piles. Prior to adding the preparations to the compost pile, an overview of how the preparations work is related to the herbal studies block that they have already completed. Explaining the details of how the preparations are made is not essential to their understanding of why we put the preparations in the pile and can distract them from the overview we are trying to establish. If you were to actually make the preparations with the student it would become real, but simply talking about the sheaths and process without doing it becomes too intellectual—they can't understand it through their reasoning. Along with practical experience in making the preparations, a physiology block might be a good time to bring in a greater level of detail about how they are made, as many of the preparations are aged in animal organs.

Another concept that is important in biodynamic agriculture is that of vitality, which can also be called "etheric" or "formative forces." The vitality of the farm is enhanced by the biodynamic practices, much like eating a healthy diet and getting enough sleep enhances the life forces of the human being. In the garden, with the high school students, we strive to build a "picture understanding" of these forces in plants, animals and the human being. Bringing the students to observation of an unseen energetic quality that they can perceive with a sense that goes beyond the physical helps develop a feel for these formative forces. An example would be when we sense that another person is tired or awake or ill or healthy. In plants it can be seen in whether the plant seems strong, vibrant and balanced in its proportions or weak and lacking vitality. This quality can also be perceived in animals, such as with a young, vibrant animal compared to an older, less energetic animal.

Another important biodynamic concept that is introduced in the garden work is that of "cosmic" and "earthly" forces. These forces originate in the spiritual world. They can't be measured with scientific instruments or perceived with our ordinary senses and can only be measured or quantified once they have an effect on matter. "Cosmic" forces are the peripheral formative forces pushing in, and "earthly" forces are the central formative forces pushing out. The forms we see in living things are a physical manifestation of this play of cosmic and earthly forces interacting. This discussion happens in the garden, where the environment serves as an example. Together we share our individual pictures of the idea of "cosmic" and "earthly" forces. With "cosmic" forces we talk about how there are effects that come from planets far away that reach the earth and have an effect on the plants. The rotational patterns of planets produce a force that affects the earth. Patterns or imprints of these forces are seen in all of nature, for example, in the geometry of petal patterns and seashell segments. In the fruiting and flowering stage of the plant, the force of the sun is a very important factor, whereas in the root and stem development, the gravitational force of the earth is more predominant in its influence. The shapes of the leaves and parts of plants are formed through the combination of these "cosmic" and "earthly" forces. For example, the yarrow leaf has a fine, frilly leaf form, which can be described as a cosmic imprinting into the outside edge of the leaf. A counter example is the nasturtium leaf with greater "earthly" forces acting on it, pushing from the center out. After pointing out these forces manifested in the phenomenon of form in the garden, our discussion goes to rest while we return to the practical aspects, the work itself. The ideas incubate in the student.

Another practical project is the stirring and spraying of Preparation 500 during the Michaelmas or Harvest Festival that comes at the end of September. While third graders are pressing apple juice and preparing a harvest dinner, ninth graders can be stirring and spraying the preparation on the land. It is good to select a group of students that are ready and interested in this next step. After receiving a picture from the teacher of their task, physically and spiritually, they are capable of understanding the responsibility they carry.

Festivals are a time to bless the land and bring the community together. What we notice and care for is then blessed by our awareness. Biodynamic practices are a way of feeding the forces of the future, which in turn, feed us.

5   The Roots of Garden Teaching

Be a gardner.
Dig a ditch,
toil and sweat
and turn the earth upside down
and seek deepness
and water the plants in time.
Continue this labor

and make sweet floods to run
and noble and abundant fruits
to spring.
Take this food and drink
and carry it to God
as your worship.
                              —*Julian of Norwich*

THE FIRST FORMAL SCHOOL garden in America was started in 1891 in Massachusetts when the majority of Americans were still living in rural areas but city populations were rising due to industrialization. Prior to this era a "school garden" as such would not have been necessary as most children came to school from self-sufficient family farms or households with vegetable gardens. They would naturally have experienced growing food within the cycle of the year at home. Even before this, the Indigenous people of this continent engaged the entire community in rituals of planting and harvesting, and gardening in a school was not a separate activity.

School gardens gained popularity between 1910 and 1920 during the Great Depression as a way to provide for the students' and their families' basic needs, and to make sure that children stayed in contact with nature. The movement grew quickly along with the Victory Garden movement during the two World Wars, again fueled by the necessity to produce more food, as precious resources were being funneled to war efforts. After World War II, with more and more people moving to larger cities with little room for school gardens, the school garden movement began to die out.

With the development of suburbs, and the resulting alienation from wild and culti-vated nature, children needed school gardening programs even more.

The school garden movement went to sleep after the end of World War II and did not wake up until the late 1960s, when the "Back to the Land" movement began fostering an interest in growing your own food. On the East Coast, Robert Rodale pioneered and popularized the concept of organic gardening and spurred a movement through books, publications, and education centers. At this time biodynamic farming was also gaining strength on the East Coast.

On the West Coast, Alan Chadwick's Student Farming Project at UC Santa Cruz trained and inspired many young people who went on to create school gardening programs. Notable among them are Thom and Patty Dunks who wrote the foundational book *Gardening with Children*. The development of school garden education has continued with the help of countless school gardening teachers, as well as Alice Waters and her work in Berkeley, California. In the 1990s Alice Waters coined the phrase, "A Garden in Every School." As a world-renowned chef, she not only wanted the children to grow the food, which they do at Berkeley's Martin Luther King Middle School Edible Schoolyard, but to cook, serve, and eat the food in a beautiful space.

This modern reappearance of the school gardening movement has been shown to awaken interest and incentive in children, even increasing school attendance and helping children to become more alert and focused on their academic studies. School garden programs have also been found to be a pathway into a deeper interest in the sciences, even as a life occupation. It cannot be overstated that school garden programs fill a void that has arisen today as agricultural family life has almost disappeared from society.

In 1979, the first Life Lab project emerged in Santa Cruz, California, and became influential in the growing school gardening movement. The program promotes gardens—both indoor and outdoor—as the "living laboratory for elementary school science." The Life Lab is a non-profit organization that provides teacher trainings and teacher manuals to support the implementation of their garden program practices.

In some pedagogical circles gardening is now seen as not only an essential physical activity that supports important learning, but also as a means of teaching healthy eating practices and exposing children to fresh fruits and vegetables that may be missing from the family meal. Alice Waters even went so far as to ask, "…are children still eating meals around the dinner table in busy households?"* In some ways schools are being asked to also fill the void of proper nourishment and dietary education that families fulfilled in prior times.

Biodynamic Garden Education

Ehrenfried Pfeiffer, a personal student of Rudolf Steiner from 1920 to 1925, seeded the biodynamic farming and education movement in the United States, first in Spring Valley, New York, then at Kimberton Farm School, in Pennsylvania, and then at his own farm in Chester, New York. After emigrating to the U.S. in 1940, his work founding the Biodynamic Farming and Gardening Association and training biodynamic educators led to many educational initiatives still thriving today. Pfeiffer studied biochemistry and was influential in examining the harmful effects of pesticides on humans. He also consulted with Rachel Carson on her influential book *Silent Spring*, which is often credited with starting the modern environmental movement. Though he did not coin it, Pfeiffer is linked to the origin of the term "organic," as its first incidence was in Lord Northbourne of Kent's book *Look to the Land*, published one year after Pfeiffer organized an agriculture conference at Lord Northbourne's estate in 1939.

At the Student Garden Project at the UC Santa Cruz campus, Alan Chadwick introduced biodynamic and French intensive methods of horticulture in the 1960s. Many of Chadwick's students were strongly influenced by his teaching and went on to develop prominent biodynamic and organic farms, education centers, and school garden programs across the country, particularly prevalent throughout California.

---

*   *Hope's Edge* by Frances Moore Lappe and Anna Lappe (TarcherPerigree, 2003)

Students at the UC Santa Cruz campus continue his work, and the center continues to be the preeminent training ground for organic farmers on the West coast.

Steiner's philosophy is abundant with references to the sacredness present in nature and the necessity for human beings to interest and involve themselves in the yearly cycles of growth, fertility, and decay. Because of these underpinnings, Waldorf schools have been special havens for school gardening programs and nature-based education. In Waldorf schools this education is seen as an integral part of the curriculum, and not as something to be added or taken away as need or funding dictates. While some Waldorf schools lack farms or gardens of their own, all Waldorf schools include outdoor, nature, and farm-based education to whatever degree is possible through field trips, walks, and nature activities.

In the U.S., Waldorf gardening programs have developed according to site, intention and the interest of parents, teachers, and board members. The curriculum has become as unique and individual as each site and community, as well as the teacher that is hired. On the East coast, there are well established gardening programs at Kimberton Waldorf School in Pennsylvania; Hawthorne Valley Waldorf School in Harlemville, New York; High Mowing Waldorf School in Wilton, New Hampshire; Green Meadow Waldorf School in Spring Valley, New York; and The Hartsbrook School in Hadley, Massachusetts. The Farm-Wise Program in Southeastern Wisconsin; Live Power Farm in rural Northern California; and Angelic Organics Learning Center outside of Chicago, Illinois all offer farm-based education programs based on the Waldorf curriculum. On the West coast many Waldorf schools have gardening programs: in California there are established programs at Summerfield Waldorf School & Farm in Santa Rosa; Sacramento Waldorf School; Santa Cruz Waldorf School; Waldorf School of the Penninsula in Los Altos; Marin Waldorf School; and Highland Hall Waldorf School in Los Angeles. Sunfield Farm & Waldorf School in Port Townsend, Washington; and Ann Arbor Waldorf School have established gardening programs.

With the recent awareness and motivation to see children learn in and from nature, and to practice the arts of gardening and farming, many schools not listed are working to start gardening programs or to find land where children can have these experiences as part of their education.

The Forest School movement, begun in Wisconsin in the 1920s, continued in Northern Europe starting in the 1950s, and is now becoming popular in many parts of the world. It has led more recently to the popularity of "Forest kindergartens." Schools such as Cedarsong on Vashon Island, Washington; The Waldorf School of Saratoga Springs' forest kindergarten in New York; Natick Community Organic Farm's Forest Gnomes class in Massachusetts; Good Earth Farm School in Austin, Texas; The Forest School of Minnesota in Minneapolis; Mother Earth School in Portland, Oregon; Little Sparrows in Maple Valley, Washington and many more are offering full-day programs held outside in whatever weather comes their way.

"All-outdoor" education is being implemented for elementary children as well. For example, the Mother Earth School has expanded their outdoor school program into the elementary years. The Earth Program at the Hawthorne Valley Waldorf School in New York has implemented "all-outdoor" education for students who thrive better with physical activity and practical skills as the basis for the school day. Some schools such as Shining Star Waldorf School in Portland, Oregon have created nature-immersion programs that run for a block or once per week for a period of time.

The related "primitive skills" and "rewilding" movements have yielded a plethora of after school, summer and holiday nature immersion and craft programs that provide students with rich nature experiences. Kroka Expeditions in New Hampshire; Weaving Earth in Northern California; the Maine Primitive Skills School; Roots School in Vermont; Headwaters Outdoor School in Santa Cruz, California; Trackers, (throughout the West); and Boulder Outdoor Survival School in Colorado are just a few of the many programs offering immersion experiences.

As a response to a growing need for curative education, craft and land-based outdoor programs incorporating gardening and farming along with other handwork have arisen in the last twenty-five years. Examples include the Mulberry School in Santa Rosa, California, and the many Camphill Communities throughout the United States, serving adults with special needs. Ruskin Mill, West of London, near Gloucester, has pioneered practical activities-based curative education for adolescents and sponsors teacher training based in practical activities as well.

As mentioned above, gardening and farm-based education programs are as diverse as their schools and farms. The movement of Waldorf based programs and other outdoor, nature based curriculums is continually growing through the collaboration of educators throughout the country. For example, Waldorf educators come together at regular events organized by Farm Based Educators Inspired by Anthroposophy (FBEIBA) and the Biodynamic Association, among others, to share and further their craft and movement.

6 Site Development & Program Design

Life begins the day you start a garden.
—Chinese Proverb

THE SITE DETERMINES THE PROGRAM: Summerfield Waldorf School and Farm serves as a good example of garden infrastructure and programming that can be developed on a large site with dedicated resources for staffing and development. The nursery through twelfth grade school occupies 32 acres of land outside of Santa Rosa, California. The campus has a seven-acre farm supplying parents, faculty, and students with weekly produce and eggs. The farm and gardens include three acres of vegetables, two acres of pasture, one acre of student gardens, a one-half acre permaculture garden, a greenhouse, an outdoor kitchen with a wood fired bread oven, and a barn housing sheep, cows, chickens, rabbits, and ducks. One hundred espaliered apple trees divide the vegetable fields and native plant hedgerows attract beneficial animals and insects.

The school has an established land trust agreement—a legal commitment to conscientious stewardship of the land—which insures that it will not be sold as a commodity and that it will be cared for in an environmentally sound and socially beneficial way. Part of the land trust is an agreement to do agricultural work with children and youth.

The size and diversity of this site allows for a broad and deep immersion into a variety of farm and garden projects. The gardening program is on the same site as the school's biodynamic farm. Here children have an opportunity to work alongside the farmer as he demonstrates many life skills that are being lost today. Students in kindergarten through third grade participate in weekly farming and gardening classes. From fourth grade through high school students attend rotating gardening blocks. In the summer there is a six-week farm camp program. In their senior year, high school students become ambassadors to gardening programs in the public schools, forming a relationship with a teacher and class and helping them to develop their garden site.

On the other end of the spectrum, when gardening in an urban or small setting, all space is precious. Raised garden beds become the focus and center of the program. Activities are embellished with stories, songs, and projects that take place in a circle of straw bales. What we think of as the limitations of a small setting stimulate greater creativity. Looking out for how to integrate what's already present with what is needed is a good practice. Others' waste will be your treasure. For example, bringing leaves to the compost is a good example of teaching how to bring something dead and dry to life again. Making a fence from branches that were just pruned shows another use of resources that would otherwise be wasted. Each garden box can have a theme, such as garden greens, fall vegetables, butterfly plants, herbs and spices and the beloved berries. Additional ideas for gardening in small spaces include vertical growing on trellises, container gardening (from one-gallon milk jugs to half wine barrels), espalier pruning of fruit trees, utilizing classroom windows to start seedlings, or keeping a worm bin.

Going offsite to a community garden can be a meaningful experience in an urban program. Some sites are within walking distance and the walk is part of the lesson. Everything along the way has a story. Sometimes the children need to be transported, along with the tools, to a farm or garden that is out of reach on foot.

Gardening Program Staffing

At small urban or suburban school gardens and in programs that do not yet have dedicated teaching staff, smaller groups of students can rotate through nutrition, language arts, and gardening activities. This can take the pressure off of one teacher having a large class in a small garden all at one time. As the children rotate through the activities everyone has a chance at all three. For example, the class teacher can take a group for a story related to gardening, while a volunteer or parent can lead a food preparation/nutrition activity and another volunteer can lead a gardening activity. This format enlarges the opportunity by broadening the focus. Parents are very willing to help with gardening classes and can lead a group with direction from the teacher. If the school has a dedicated gardening teacher but the gardening space is small, then part of the class can be left with the main teacher to allow for rotation. When working with volunteers, it is important to take the time to talk them through their activity and have all the materials they will need on hand to be well organized before the children arrive.

Many schools have parent volunteers who staff the gardening program. In that case, careful communication between parent leaders and the class teacher is essential for a good flow. Teacher/volunteer planning sessions are essential, as questions about pedagogical and classroom management issues will be ongoing. It is ideal if the teacher or parent can link the gardening activity of the day to the season or to the classroom curriculum.

Funding Your Program

One of the most sustainable ways to keep your program funded is to approach your Board of Directors or College of Teachers with a budget proposal. They need to know that the farming and gardening program is a marketing tool that will attract parents to choose to enroll their children in your school, rather than another school that does not have that program. Parents of younger children are keen to see animals that children can interact with on a school campus. A produce stand is also a marketing draw and can supplement funds (though it may not fund the program in a significant way). A further step would be creating an all-school lunch program using produce from the garden or farm that can actually generate income above expenses. Parents love not having to make lunches and are willing to pay for a healthy school lunch.

Having a summer farm camp can be a real moneymaker and is a wonderful way to get necessary gardening work done in the summer as well as being a service to parents and students. Summer programs are generally one of the most profitable programs in a school.

If your school has a large enough garden or farm, another funding source can be an annual farm fee for the entire student body, similar to how classroom supplies are often funded. A suggested amount could be anywhere from $75 to $150 per child per year. The farm fee is a fee that helps underwrite the expenses that go along with sustaining a pedagogical farm, which means that the first priority of the farm is to be a learning environment for the students—the farm is an economic venture secondarily. Otherwise, the farmer would be too busy managing the farm business without time to work with the students and communicate and coordinate with other educators. Once the priority of the farm is designated as pedagogical, it shifts the mission and creates a space to engage the students. It is always more time-consuming to work with students than to just do the work yourself! Leaders among the faculty, administration, and parent body must understand this. The trade off is that the students gain real life experiences that they wouldn't get otherwise. Income from produce sales are certainly one stream of income supporting the program, but administrators and board members must be shown a way to understand that the farm or garden is an educational program on par with other pedagogical programs such as the early childhood program, grades program, high school program, specialty subjects, and after school programs.

Grants are helpful for specific projects, but the school must value the necessity of the gardening program and fund the salary for the teacher(s). One way of looking at the gardening program is that a classroom space is not needed, and once the program is in place, it actually "produces," rather than "uses" supplies. While it may have the lowest budget, it yields essential lessons that will benefit the students lifelong.

As a group, gardening teachers need to support each other by holding regular meetings to discuss and develop curriculum and self-define the role of gardening programs and teachers.

Donations

Acquiring materials and supplies can be a big challenge. There are many opportunities for donations, and obtaining them takes time. The process involves developing relationships with donors and knowing what you need. It's helpful to remember that for business owners, giving is often an aspect of their mission. Cultivating a sense of worthiness will help those gifts come more readily. Local nurseries, lumber yards, hardware stores, and garden centers are happy to donate, but they usually need a request letter on school letterhead with the school's tax identification number as well. Create a template donation request letter that is easy to adapt for different needs and businesses. Carry an extra letter with you in case you encounter an opportunity unexpectedly. Sending a thank you letter and inviting donors to garden related events is the right thing to do and encourages more collaboration.

Grants & Fundraising

Small grants tend to be easier to write and qualify for and can provide ongoing funds for projects or one-time infrastructure needs. Fundraisers that the students participate in, such as plant sales, bake sales, and selling herbal product can also build up money for special purchases. There are many organizations and businesses looking to give money to gardening projects. It's worth the time and effort it takes to connect with these funders. Most grant funders will ask for a report on the results of your work, so be sure to budget time for this after the funds have been spent. Be aware that large grants of money come with a significant amount of paperwork, reporting, time, and energy.

Developing a School Garden Site Over Time

Your greatest tool in developing your site is your imagination. The beauty of this is that the process of transforming your site *is* the gardening program. A garden is in a continual state of transformation. This is an important concept to keep alive in your own mind, because a "perfect garden" is not the goal. Meaningful activity with children and community members that enhances their relationship with nature is the true objective. A practical way of working that pairs garden development needs with curriculum objectives is to make a list of the projects needed, and then organize them according to age appropriateness (see chapters 8–11 for examples).

Certain projects need more time and effort than the children can provide during gardening class, or than what the teacher can accomplish during allotted non-teaching hours. Parent/community workdays are a good way to get hard work done in a short amount of time. Parents are enthusiastic about participating because the workday is a learning opportunity for them. It's important to be well organized, have tools available, and prepare a well-thought-out list of tasks. With many hands, work will be accomplished faster than you think and people want to feel that their time is well used. Take time to give in-depth explanations to the workers so that they feel valued as a part of the project. Appointing one parent to work with any young children who have been brought along on the workday can be a real help.

If you are starting with a blank slate, like a lawn or weed patch, you can sheet mulch as a first step in developing your garden. Cover the area with wet cardboard or newspaper to smother any weeds. Layer organic material such as straw, grass clippings, leaves, compost, and wood chip mulch. These will decompose over time building topsoil and attract worms, while keeping weeds from growing. The sheet mulch starts to create a visual picture of what's coming.

A site that develops slowly will have greater results. As long as you maintain your forward motion, the wait is worthwhile. If we wish to truly educate the children, their engagement and the process, not the product, are the goal. If you start small, and develop slowly over time, your chances of sustaining the program are greater because it's hard to build and maintain simultaneously.

Animals

Animals offer a transformative opportunity for children to nurture and care for a living creature. They necessitate more attention for their upkeep and more protection than plants do, but fill a large place in the gardening program. Animal manures provide exceptional nutrients and demonstrate the value of recycling waste. A scheduled visit of an animal from a child's home can fill the niche if you are not able to have your own.

Some considerations include weekend and summer care and adequate housing to protect against predators and weather conditions. Animals must not be allowed to become too hot or cold and they need a regular feeding schedule and nighttime safety. The cycle of life and death is a real experience on the farm, as animals will come to the end of their productivity and sometimes be slaughtered, or die of natural causes. This is of concern especially with smaller animals such as laying hens with shorter life cycles. Children can receive this information as a pedagogical story that helps them deal with the concept of death, which they will certainly encounter in the future. These are questions to look at before deciding whether to have animals.

Site Assessment

An initial site assessment is necessary so that you can make a long-range plan. Use the following as a checklist for assessing the important features of your site.

Rural / urban considerations

- In rural and some urban settings fencing must be installed to protect against wildlife entering the garden
- In an urban setting consider having smaller animals such as chickens or rabbits
- Containers, barrels, and raised bed boxes are all useful in urban settings
- It is important to form positive relationships with neighbors. This can decrease the danger of vandalism.

Land formation and slope

- Identify slopes in order to accommodate water runoff during the rainy season

- Determine wet and dry spots so that they are used appropriately
- If possible, have the older students help you in assessing the positive and negative qualities of a variety of garden sites

HOURS OF SUNLIGHT AND ASPECT

- Consider the aspect of the land: southwest aspect is considered the best, while northern aspect will reduce sunlight in the fall, winter and early spring
- Spend time in the garden recording the sunlight and calculate if it is sufficient (six hours minimum)
- Estimate how the sunlight will shift through the seasons
- Consider the effect of deciduous and evergreen trees on the sunlight
- Buildings absorb and reflect heat back to plants. This has an effect on the garden
- Shade is not impossible to work with, but limits the choice of plantings. Vegetables will not grow well in shade

QUALITY OF SOIL

- Investigate the history of the site and its uses to determine if there might be chemical or heavy metal contamination
- Test for possible soil contamination and seek professional guidance if necessary
- Take soil nutrient and texture samples from a number of spots in the garden as soil can vary widely. Nutrients provide for plant's needs, while texture affects drainage. Both can be worked with as long as you know what you have

GARDEN LAYOUT

- Take time developing your garden layout on paper and expect it to change
- Consider the movement of people in the space and how to facilitate it. Consider that the heaviest traffic is related to entry and exit points, travel to tool sheds and to the compost piles. Make sure garden paths can accommodate wheelbarrows or garden carts
- Prioritize components that your site can manage. For example, you most likely

need a gathering space but might not need a cob oven

- Tool storage is essential and will protect and organize your tools. This gives form and intention to the students. Lock your tool shed when not in use. Have a method of cleaning tools that is clear to the children and happens at the end of each lesson
- A cooking facility can be as simple as cutting boards and a knife, or as complex as a full kitchen. Consider shade for cooking and water for drinking and hand washing. A picnic table or piece of plywood on straw bales can serve well
- A gathering place is needed to start the lesson and give a picture of the workday. This should be a comfortable place so that you can keep the students' attention. Many gardening activities need a work table and shade. Trees are nice but umbrellas suffice
- Fencing is a large endeavor and must be thoroughly thought through and funded before you embark. If it is absolutely necessary, and funds aren't available, make a long-term plan. Use temporary fencing as needed until you can accomplish the larger project
- Compost piles need to be accessible on all sides and need partial shade. It is ideal if you can make your own compost, yet there are times when it must be purchased. Be sure to research the ingredients. Organic certified compost is preferred
- Erecting a greenhouse can be a long-term project and a valuable asset. Site it in full sun with an adequate foundation. Small greenhouses can be built of wood or PVC pipes and greenhouse plastic. If even a small greenhouse is not an option, propagation mats and fluorescent lights can be used indoors. Propagation is an important lesson to share with the children, so plan it into your curriculum program
- An ample water source is essential for filling watering cans, hoses, or supplying drip irrigation or sprinklers. If you have a choice, locate a hose bib centrally with additional hose bibs in other locations. Have a safe source of drinking water for the children. Whenever possible, install a rainwater catchment system

Program Design

The first questions to think about are the age of the children, how much time can they spend in the garden and who is teaching them. First assess the number of hours and the ages of the students you will be teaching. Next make a list of all the activities appropriate for each age. Now, organize the list seasonally. This is one way to form and order the ongoing activities. From there, you can break it down even further into materials needed, opening verse or story, skills, and closing verse or song for each class period.

A weekly or daily visioning walk—to see what is calling to be done, to notice problems, to glean new projects, to assess water needs, etc.—is essential. This walk is like a meditation—a time to perceive what the garden needs. This is the practice for connecting the work that the children will do with the present needs seen in the garden. This helps to prioritize tasks. Stay open to the possibility that the vision will continually change.

Developing relationships is important. For example, the maintenance person may be able to lend tools, can help advise where to have materials delivered, or can help think through building projects. Building relationships can encourage other teachers to use the garden to enhance a lesson that they are teaching. Maybe you have an abundance of lettuce to share. This can be a joyful collaboration that builds community.

It is important to weave themes from the classroom into the garden curriculum. Ask teachers for their lesson plans for the school year and have a brief meeting to coordinate lessons and discuss the needs of the children as a class and individually. Collaboration with the music teacher can also be helpful, as there are many work songs and farm related songs available. Singing in the garden unites and inspires the children.

There must be a plan for summer care or your hard work during the school year may be lost. The garden is a part of the school facility, and, similar to other parts, must be maintained year-round. You can offer a weekly gardening day to parents and students, or even a summer gardening program for which you can charge money.

Another option is a rotating schedule of parent volunteers who water and weed and may harvest crops if they wish. Staffed summer garden maintenance hours are ideal. The garden teacher, students, and maintenance staff are all good staffing options.

Make a plan for the use of the produce harvested from the garden. Some can be donated or sold, but the more that the children eat the deeper the meaning of the task will be for them. A cooking project each week is a great use of produce. Cooking is essential to create a full circle experience in the garden. This demands extra time, help, and planning. The end result is always worthwhile. The children always remember what they have eaten in the garden. Children are also excited to take produce home.

Unless you have a summer program, avoid crops that will ripen in the summer. Plant spring-maturing crops such as berries, asparagus, and garlic. In addition to spring crops, plant crops that will be harvested in the fall such as cucumbers, tomatoes, pumpkins, green beans, and summer squash (this requires a plan for tending to crops during the summer break). Crops that can be grown and harvested in both spring and fall include lettuce, herbs, carrots, beets, kale, chard, broccoli, peas, and radishes*. Children love to harvest tree fruit, so even one apple tree will be appreciated and well-tended.

Field trips help the students gain perspective, especially to established farms with farm animals. Take time to research local farms and build relationships that can lead to yearly visits. For example, find a goat farm where they make cheese, an herb farm growing healing herbs or a butterfly garden. These also expand and inspire new ideas for your site.

Tools

Without the tools, nothing gets done. Having well-crafted tools that are age appropriate is essential. It is much better to have a strong tool that will not break than many cheap tools that fall apart. Children can form an intimacy with the tools that they use

---

*   Planting times are dependent on your climate.

and we must help them to develop a relationship of respect, care, and skill. Make sure that the children have a clear picture of a tool's proper use. Explain this before you hand them the sacred object. A demonstration by the teacher is essential in creating this picture. If you have a variety of ages of children, different size tools are necessary. Children in early childhood through fourth grade should use the smaller tools, and fifth through twelfth graders can use the larger ones.

REAL WORK IN RELATIONSHIP TO TOOLS

In daily life, children need to be engaged in chores—at home and at school—which they are responsible for, and that are essential to daily life. Each task has a meaning and purpose. Engagement in the task helps the student feel needed and part of something essential. The essential "need to be needed" is a key part of human experience. When this quality of purpose is missing, other things may fill the space. A sense of restlessness can lead to trouble. There is a moral quality that comes from the rhythm of taking up chores. An example that comes to mind is cleaning up after the work is done. Collecting, cleaning, and returning all tools to their proper place is an important part of the class, and only when all tools are accounted for can we have our closing verse and/or review. This care shows a willingness to be true to the needs of the situation, to ourselves, and to our community.

WHAT IS A TOOL?

A tool is an extension of the hand or foot. Every tool has logic and the student must discover the logic inherent in it. The job to be done determines the tool. In gardening, the student is led into practical skills that come from a lawfulness that exists outside of the human being, and is connected to the archetypal movement and ergonomics of each tool. This lawfulness teaches the student how to use a tool. The interaction between tool and the world becomes a series of adjustments as the student observes the results. Tools challenge the student to move and to use their will. This interaction can be hard and demanding. In using a saw, applying more pressure does not work. The saw has its demands that must be met by the user.

Essential Garden Tools

- Square edge spade: used for heavy digging, cutting soil into clods and cutting straight edges for a bed. Also useful for double digging

- Round point shovel: used to break stiff ground, loosen soil and dig a hole. The "bowl" shaped shovel can hold and move material

- Digging fork: used for loosening the soil and for weed removal. Goes straight into the soil with the help of the foot pushing on the edge

- Pitch fork/hay fork: used to lift lightweight material such as leaves or straw to be moved. Never pushed into the ground

- Krail: used to move material such as manure or compost by pulling towards oneself

- Hand pruners: used to remove dead growth on plants, and to cut flowers and prune trees, berries, roses, etc.

- Loppers: used to cut woody branches that are too thick for the hand pruners

- Trowel: used to make holes for transplanting seedlings

- Hoe: used for weeding. Cuts into soil by digging in and drawing towards oneself. Purchase hoes with a correct ergonomic blade angle for weeding

- Heavy headed hoe: the blade is at a right angle to the handle. It is much stronger and can be used by older children and used with more force for chopping

- Hand hoe: used for precise cultivation and weeding in rows and beds

- Hand-weeder: another precise cultivating tool with a triangular edge to get more delicate action

- Cultivator: a long handled tool with a triangular head for precise loosening of soil around plants

- Watering can: should be sized for children to be able to lift and pour. Use of hoses by children can easily get out of control

- Steel rake, bow rake or hard rake: used for moving soil while shaping beds and for gathering up heavier materials

- Leaf rake: used for moving lighter materials such as leaves, straw and grass clippings

- Wheelbarrow or garden cart: size should be dependent on the age of the children
- Sun hat: sun hats are helpful for keeping children from getting overheated
- Gloves: help students protect their hands to prevent blisters. Gloves must be sized for children. The hand is the original tool

For older children:

- Mattock: used for digging out stubborn roots and loosening compacted soil
- Scythe: used for hand-cutting high grass
- Small sledge: used for pounding in stakes or rebar
- Pruning saw: used for cutting larger branches

7 Preparing Food from the Garden

Love is a fruit in season at all times and within the reach of every hand.
—*Mother Theresa*

ONCE THE PLANTS BEGIN producing food, a new and welcome activity comes into play: harvesting, cooking, and eating. Children begin to eat food that they never wished to try before because they now pull it from the earth, wash it, and prepare it themselves. As full participants in the process, they develop a sense for taste and quality. Through gardening with children, we are educating them about the love of good food. As time and site allow, students, with the help of their teacher, can be given the privilege and responsibility of cooking a snack to be shared at the end of class, something that is seasonally available and simple, yet tasty. The social quality of sharing food together builds a sense of community in the class. Eating the fruits of our labor brings the work of gardening full circle and connects the student with purposeful activity.

Kindergarten, First & Second Grades

In the kindergarten there is often the smell of something wonderful cooking. The child is fed through the sense of smell. The snack in the kindergarten, often warm, is more like a small meal, and returns the enormous energy that they have expended in their morning play. It is a time when they are most hungry and willing to sit at the table and enjoy the comfort of a meal. Many kindergartens serve the same snacks each week, for instance, Monday is "rice day." If the kindergarten has a kitchen, the children can help prepare the food. They can rotate in and out of helping, coming to do a part and leaving when others want a turn or when they feel done. They are driven by their interest and their desire to help and to imitate the actions of the teacher.

On a kindergarten garden day, a good option is to press apples and make juice that can be enjoyed cold in the fall and warm in the winter. Apples can be cut, dried, and saved for spring. This constant connection with the apple in its many forms is just the right treat at the end of the garden lesson. For a quick snack apple slices are always a joy. Fresh carrots, pod peas, or radishes tasted right in the garden are simple and immediate, while the sweetness of an apple is a real treat for a kindergarten child.

First and second grade lessons move more quickly and some days there is only time for the dried apples on the return to class or a few raspberries from the bushes. If time allows, harvest something from the garden with the children such as carrots or pod peas. After washing the produce, we sit together in a circle, say a blessing, and allow time for each child to eat their treasure before heading back to class. As young children of this age are newly learning to work, receiving something delicious from the garden as often as possible is exciting and motivating.

Third, Fourth & Fifth Grades

In the third grade, cooking is a large part of the curriculum. They learn skills for food preparation such as cutting safely with knives, what sizes vegetables need to be cut into, and which foods go together to create a meal. Now fire or heat is used to transform raw vegetables into soups and they can engage in the whole process. They learn to use measuring utensils and read recipes. Sauteing is a new-found skill, involving time and heat. Up until now they have helped prepare parts of the recipe. Now they are at the forefront, stirring it over the flame. They build community as they all wash, chop, cook and share a meal together.

As part of fourth grade geography it is important to recognize the cultures of the people who historically lived on the land and their food ways. Acorns were a mainstay for the indigenous people of what is today California, and processing acorns into meal, mush, and bread can bring an appreciation and taste for this valuable resource as they experience regionally and historically significant ways of eating. The fourth grade gardening curriculum is less focused on cooking since they are very busy with their animal husbandry tasks.

In the fifth grade, supporting the study of Ancient India, it is fun to cook an Indian feast using fruits and vegetables from the farm and garden. Recipes such as potato curry, spicy green beans, cucumber raita, pear and apple chutney, biryani rice, and poori are all prepared by the students, with help from parents. Before eating, the children change into Indian attire and sit down to enjoy the fruits of their labor.

Sixth, Seventh & Eighth Grades

Cooking touches the adolescent by engaging the senses, stimulating an interest in the food, and developing skills. Cooking is a type of alchemy. It is one way to find the "magic key to the heart of the student." Cooking out of the garden can help adolescents make better food choices and even inspire them to prepare things at home for their families. The culture of eating is universal and students today are more interested in taking a role in preparing food.

This is the age when a small group of students can work together to independently prepare a snack for the whole class. Often the students plan a snack and bring the additional ingredients and recipe from home. The teacher can help by reviewing the ingredients and making sure it is healthy. They love to bake, and low sugar items like scones or muffins are good. Dips like hummus or guacamole are also fun, and can include farm vegetables. Quesadillas and pizza are popular and use all kinds of skills and ingredients such as onions, broccoli, garlic, kale, and tomatoes from the garden. If the garden does not have access to a kitchen, simple snacks such as popcorn, which can be homegrown, or baked potatoes in a solar oven, or even sun tea can be very satisfying.

Salads are fun; topped with edible flowers and grated carrots and beets they become a beautiful and refreshing snack.

High School

In high school the students often continue to choose the recipe and lead the cooking activity. Through elective classes, the students are offered a block on cooking and nutrition. What is a healthy diet? What foods give which kinds of nutritional values? How do the different systems of the body function? What herbs help heal which kinds of ailments? Learning to properly cut and cook vegetables from the garden, make healthy desserts, soups, muffins, and sauces all give opportunities for the observation and transformation of substances with fire. A real wood fire, either in a fire circle or in a brick bread oven gives an opportunity to have a direct experience with this primal element. Baking potatoes or making pizza helps the student observe the different qualities of taste and the differences in cooking times.

In high school, the focus is predominantly on vegetarian main dishes, breakfast items, and salads, using many of the fruits, vegetables, and herbs from the farm. Quality of ingredients is stressed, as is proper cutting, timing, cooking techniques, seasoning, and final presentation. With skills gained in class, students prepare a complete meal at home, documenting all steps from recipes to shopping to the final product. When cooking in class, all students are engaged in preparing the recipes. They work in groups of three or four, building social skills and ultimately sharing a bountiful meal.

These cooking activities can lead to service projects such as making products for sale in the school community as a fundraiser. Other ideas include:

- Drying herbs and then grinding them with salt in a mortar and pestle can produce a lovely herbal salt
- Chopping cabbage and fermenting with salt can make a tasty sauerkraut
- Cooking apples down and learning how to preserve the applesauce in canning jars
- Cooking and preserving elderberry syrup
- Cooking and canning salsa and tomato sauce

Seasonal Activities: K–12

8 Nursery & Kindergarten

The child needs to be led into unification of all life in all directions, beginning in himself, with his neighbor, with society and with nature and her laws.
—Friedrich Froebel

THE YOUNG CHILD up until the age of seven is most active in their will forces through their physicality and boundless energy. Their emotional and intellectual capacities are, for the most part, dormant. Unlike thoughts and feelings, which develop in full force later, the realm of the will is "outside" the child, in their limbs and actions. Therefore, the young child lives more in the periphery. This can be hard to see because it is so different from the adult, who sees herself as a focused point in physical space. For example, young children are often not even aware that they are the cause of their bodily movements. We can see this clearly if we compare a three-year-old, who is just barely able to say "I do it" instead of "me do it," to an adolescent, who most certainly has a sense of themselves as an individual with thoughts and, of course, very strong feelings of likes and dislikes.

As mentioned earlier, the young child learns through imitation. While an older child may be more strongly influenced by their teacher through the feeling and intellectual realms, communication with the young child works best when it is action-oriented and functional. Direct, objective speech and clear commands that stay in the present moment are wonderfully effective, while cajoling, intellectualizing or moralizing just confuse and can lead to emotional outbursts. It is also helpful to have compassion for the fact that the child isn't yet fully in command of their body and will forces. Objectifying hands and feet can help the child to accept your guidance, as in, "Are your hands having a hard time being gentle?" For the young child, the urge to strike out and hit another child doesn't pass through the filter of right and wrong. It feels to them as if their hand wanted to hit, not them. The gentle instruction, "hands are for working and loving," or, "our hands are gentle now," hits home, while the moral argument simply confounds.

In addition to simple, functional commands, action is the best way to teach the young child, who will most likely follow your actions wordlessly, or say, "me too!" and run to join you. Do not explain with many words or concepts, or ask whether they prefer the blue or red watering can. There is plenty of time to get into concepts, preferences, and right and wrong later. At this age, forcing a child to go into their mind, searching for an answer for something they can't possibly know, takes their energy away from developing physically, something that is essential for strong and healthy formation of the internal organs and bodily functions. Time spent in healthy outdoor gross and fine motor activities develops their will capacities instead of channeling energy into an intellect that is not yet ready to bloom.

Nursery and kindergarten-aged children have an inherent relationship with nature. Taking a walk each week in a garden, farm, or nature area, always following the same route, allows the seasonal rhythms and changes to take center stage, and the children to relax into the well-known. They especially like entering a garden gate, feeling the boundary and feeling protected. They enjoy walking on winding paths, over bridges, sitting on benchesm and going into little huts. Fallen trees are perfect balancing beams. They will make excellent use of teepees, arbors, and sunflower houses made with old crops. They forage for food, like birds, and even in the fall they will pick and eat the dried sweet grapes that are turning to raisins on the vine. Seeds, leaves, pods, acorns, bark, and moss all have unlimited potential in imaginative play and are good building materials for fairy homes. They love to find precious objects along the way, and its handy to bring a basket for these found treasures. The following verse captures the mood:

But who comes here on scampering feet?
Looking for acorns and nuts to eat?

Whisky, friskey, hippety hop.
Up he goes to the tall tree top.
Whirly, twirly, round and round.
Down he scampers to the ground.

Curly, furly, oh, what a tail.
Tall as a feather, broad as a sail.
Where's his supper? In the shell.
Snappity, crackity, out it fell.

Gardening with the young child can simply take place during the outdoor play time within the school day and be led by the nursery or kindergarten teacher, or be a special class period within the week. During outdoor playtime, the changing seasons are very apparent to the young child. As soon as they step out of the classroom door there is something new and different. The air, sounds, and temperature all begin to affect this "newly hatched chick." Rain pants, rain boots, hats and gloves in the winter; sun hats and a light jacket in the spring must be eased into and accounted for. The teacher can now bring out the tools and as she begins the work, some are eager to join. Some can follow their urge for sandcastle building, while others are still in their imaginative play. The teacher must be aware of all that is going on, while students weave in and out of an array of outdoor activities. The outdoor activities give a time to breath, but not to the point of wildness and roughhousing. The proper engagement of heart, head, and limbs will make for respectful work and play. The well-grounded work of the teacher—sweeping or raking the path, filling watering cans with water, harvesting edible pod peas or pulling weeds for the compost—brings forth parallel activities from the children. There is no need to say, "It's time to weed," a simple tug and an exclamation, "I got the root!" entices nearby children to try it.

In the play yard, water play is important, and in the garden this can be a rain barrel, a watering can, a pond, or a birdbath (but never a hose as they don't know how to control it). All creatures appreciate a place to bathe and drink. Finding a frog or a toad is a wonderful adventure of looking under rocks and in wet places. In the permaculture garden we have swales that catch water in the winter and a rock-filled ravine where the water can run away in the heaviest of storm; this is a great meeting place of earth and water. The kindergarten child makes a slow journey from one amazing place to another with all senses open to the natural world.

Primary Activities for Nursery and Kindergarten

If the nursery or kindergarten class comes to the school garden or farm, the session begins with a short circle song or game. The early childhood teacher often leads the gardening class since they hold the relationship with the children and the budget may not allow for a separate gardening teacher at this age. If there is a gardening teacher leading the class, having the nursery or kindergarten teacher there helps to keep the form and put the children at ease so that the gardening teacher can focus on their teaching.

For the young child, tasting from the garden creates an immediate positive connection. The first opportunity for this is simply beginning each gardening session with a walkabout on the farm, looking at what's there and tasting a few morsels. Harvest edible pod peas, carrots, or radishes in the spring; beans, cherry tomatoes, and lemon cucumbers in the late spring or fall, and then eat straight from the garden. The children's imaginations are engaged when you feed kale and lettuce to the "baby goats" who are hungrily bleating. The children may then run off to further imaginative "goat" play. A mood of reverence can be cultivated if after each child pulls her peas from the vine, you sit in a circle and give thanks prior to eating your bites.

Other opportunities for tasting the bounty abound: pick fresh mint or other herbs to make a pot of tea on the spot (with a spot of honey of course) or set a jar of sun tea to brew; pick and eat fresh strawberries, raspberries or apples to taste right then and there; sample the edible borage and nasturtium flowers. The teacher must carry a pocketknife to cut up larger fruit to hand tastes all around. Many of these activities, even if extremely simple, quickly become a repeated moment in each gardening class, building the rhythm that so nourishes the young child.

There needs to be clear guidelines for the young ones regarding eating from the garden. The teacher must be clear with setting these boundaries. We have a "pick after asking" rule. This helps us to ensure that plants are not uprooted unintentionally or over-harvested so they cannot possibly regrow. Young children cannot make these judgments, so a quick "may I harvest peas?" leads to proper supervision. It is important to avoid any poisonous plants around young children as they may disregard or forget our direction and put something in their mouth. Plants like foxglove, lantana, vinca, poison hemlock, and others should be kept away from young children*. Having a rule of asking the teacher to eat from the garden also helps to avoid accidents if a hemlock weed happens to go unnoticed in the corner of the field.

After the garden walkabout, lead the children in daily garden chores that engage the will forces. Chores can take place each class and give the children the opportunity to relax into routine. Chores such as feeding the worms, feeding the chickens and gathering eggs, combing the bunnies, or watering garden plants with watering cans to "give broth to the root children" can be engaged in by the entire group. Direction from the teacher such as, "It's April's turn to gather eggs today," " Jonah will get the bunny out of its cage, or, "Lila will hold him on her lap and Adrian will comb," give form and security that all will have a turn at some point.

After chores, a main activity is next. Each main gardening activity can be engaged in for multiple weeks, as the children are again able to sink into the rhythm. In the fall, gathering apples from the lower branches as well as wind-fall fruit to take back to the classroom can lead to a number of activities. These include helping the classroom

---

*   Consult a full list of poisonous plants for your area.

teacher cut and dry apples to store in jars for the daily snack, baking apple butter in the oven or cooking apple sauce on the stove. Applesauce could even be cooked in the garden in a solar oven. Using an apple press, make juice in the autumn for the children to drink just before returning to their classroom. Safety is very important because the grinder is very dangerous; with supervision, the children can take turns throwing apples into the hopper from a safe distance.

The children love to pull plants that have gone to seed (sometimes standing as tall as they are) and haul them to the compost pile. Weeds can be pulled and brought to feed the chickens. Eggs or root vegetables can be washed in large tubs of water for the weekly farm stand. If you grow storage crops, another autumn task that can be carried over many weeks is shelling corn or beans. In late fall, we put the garden to bed by putting "blankets" of straw on "Mother Earth." It is time for her to rest during the cold winter. A wonderful activity just before tucking the straw into the beds is to plant the "bulb children," such as daffodils, narcissus, freesia, *Crocosmia* (also a good pollinator and basketry plant), and tulips. The "bulb children" will be the first to awaken in the spring and this brings a healthy expectancy to the children.

In the winter, the children can help gather the orchard prunings to take to the brush pile. And of course a number of choice sticks and branches will make it back to the classroom. A magical activity on a really cold day is to lay a fire in the fire circle and roast veggie dogs. Before lighting the fire, each child must find a suitable stick to be whittled at the end by the teacher before popping on a hot dog. You could also roast potatoes or other veggies in foil in the coals.

Early Spring can bring an opportunity to come and visit the newly born lambs or other animals. We must "find our quiet" and the children show an inborn reverence with these young gentle creatures. Pulling spring weeds mirrors the exuberance of the season as we vigorously work at removing the roots, carefully shaking the earth back into the beds, and bringing them to the compost pile. Spring is time to plant the flower garden and to seed veggies such as peas, beans, root vegetables, and greens.

The children can place the "seed children," who long to be held by their mother, carefully in the earth and firm the soil around the roots of seedlings such as lettuce, cooking greens, and flowers. Smaller seeds can be placed in the ground by the teacher and covered and firmed over by the children.

The class can close with a snack brought from the classroom in a wagon, or prepared from the garden, and then a simple closing circle with a movement activity or verse and goodbye, if gardening teacher led the session.

Curriculum Examples

YEAR-ROUND PROJECTS

Sand, Wood & Stones (Year-Round)

What you will need:

- River rocks or other stones
- Tree branches
- Logs (approximately 2–3 inches in diameter)
- Sand pile
- Moss
- Leaf pile
- Hand trowels

What to do:

During an outdoor free-play time in the garden, have these materials available so that children can move them and create imaginary gardens. The teacher is present to make sure that the imaginative play is safe and socially appropriate. Just being with the natural materials and the elements in an unstructured way is the children's way of learning.

Composting Kindergarten Kitchen Scraps (Year-Round)

What you will need:

- A bucket with a lid

- Kitchen Scraps
- A compost pile or worm bin

What to do:

Gather food scraps as you do your cooking tasks in the classroom. Bring to the compost pile or worm pile. Allow the children to take part in feeding the food to the pile. Empty and wash the bucket daily. Make sure that your compost pile receives enough water and carbon rich material (to balance the kitchen scraps). Harvest the fully decomposed compost when ready and take it with the children in buckets to the garden beds so the children see the daily transformation of food into soil and back to the garden again.

Worm Composting (Year-Round)

Worm castings are fully digested organic matter transformed into humus through the digestion of the worms. Humus causes our soils to be fertile at the most basic level. In addition to being a storehouse of nutrients for plant roots, the humus can hold up to 900% more water than sandy soil. We are dependent on worms for our very lives! Caring for worms and then harvesting their manure (castings) to build vital humus stores in our garden beds is a wonderful activity for all ages, but especially for the young child. Worm composting can be set up on a very small scale in a small bin or on a large scale in a large bin, trough, or windrow. Frequent feeding, watering, and shade are necessary to keep the worms happy.

What you will need:
- A worm bin
- Shredded paper (newspaper or other non-toxic, non-glossy/waxy paper)
- Raw fruit and vegetable scraps, coffee grounds and filters, tea leaves, etc.
- A tarp

What to do:
- Gather scraps of fresh fruits and vegetables in a bucket. While worms will happily

eat many cooked foods, since these foods can attract rodents, it is better to use pre-consumer waste

- Allow the scraps to sit in the bucket for a week so that the composting action of bacteria will partially break down the food (worms don't have teeth to bite hard bits). Chopping food up into smaller pieces can also be helpful

- Add scraps on a weekly basis to the worm bin and top with a layer of moistened shredded paper. Keeping the empty space between the food and the lid filled with shredded paper will decrease the chance of flies breeding

- Each week, find, hold and look at worms with the children just prior to feeding them

- When the worm bin gets full, stop feeding for a few weeks until the food has been digested

- To harvest worm castings, form a pyramid shape with the castings on a tarp. With hands or trowels, shave a few inches of castings off of the surface of the pyramid and put into a bucket or container. As the worms become exposed to the light, they will retreat further down inside the pyramid. Continue to take off the castings in layers, until you have a core of castings. The worms can then be returned to the bin to start the feeding process over again

- An alternate method is to place food only on one side of the bin for a few weeks. The worms will migrate to the new food and you can harvest the castings from the uninhabited side

- The castings can be used to amend planting areas. They should be worked into the soil since if they are left as a layer on top, they will form a crust as they dry

- The castings are very high in nitrogen, so they need to be mixed into garden soil and used sparingly. Never grow in straight castings as they are too concentrated

Fall Projects

Seed Saving (Fall)

Seed saving is a wonderful indoor or outdoor activity for the autumn or winter. The children love to pop bean, pea, and brassica seeds from the pods and shell corn from the cob. Working with larger seeds develops their fine motor skills. Smaller seeds can be threshed by placing them on a tarp or sheet, and "dancing" on the dry plant matter. The children can pick the dry pods and branches out after the "dance." Perhaps the teacher or older children will complete the threshing by sieving the seeds through screens.

What you will need:

- Seeds still in their pods, cobs, or seed-heads
- Tarp or sheet
- Bowls or trays
- Jars for storing seeds
- Container to transport dry plant matter to the compost

What to do:

For large seeds:

- Set up seats around a table or on a blanket on the floor or ground
- Place a bowl for the seeds within reach of each child
- Place a container for the dry plant matter within reach of each child
- Show the children how to pop open the pods or push the corn kernels off the cob and where to put seeds and the pod when finished

For small seeds:

- Place a large sheet or tarp on the floor or ground
- Have the children help you carefully place the dry plant matter with the seeds in it into one half of the sheet or tarp, then fold the other half over so that the seeds won't spill out
- Take turns "dancing" or stomping on the dry plants
- After everyone has had a turn, lift the sheet or tarp off the plant matter and everyone

can pick out the branches and plant matter to bring to the compost

- Put the seeds in a jar or bowl for further threshing and cleaning at a later time

Song: "Mother Earth" (*Pentatonic Song Book*)

Winter Projects

Honor Water (Winter)

No drop of water should be wasted or lost and all waters should be protected and revered. There are many ways to honor and transform water, especially in the rainy season. Capturing water in buckets, barrels, or watering cans is a way of caring for the earth, bringing this great resource to the plants that need it. A barrel that gathers water year round would need a fine mesh screen on the top in order to stop mosquitoes from breeding. The children go to the barrel to access the water, dipping it out or using a tap. They are allotted a certain amount and must put it where it is needed. Find a way to communicate the importance of capturing this precious resource to the children, such as: "this is our sky water," or calling attention to how the barrel fills when it rains. Rain dances, poems, songs, and games all bring joy to the holy water. Wynstones Press books are a great resource for finding such poems and songs. An example follows:

> *THE ELF AND THE DORMOUSE*
> *Under a toadstool crept a wee elf, out of the rain to shelter himself.*
> *Under a toadstool sound asleep, sat a big dormouse all in a heap.*
> *Trembled the wee elf, frightened, and yet, fearing to fly away lest he get wet.*
>
> *To the next shelter—maybe a mile! Suddenly the wee elf smiled a wee smile.*
> *Tugged till the toadstool toppled in two. Holding it over him gaily he flew.*
> *Soon he was safe home, dry as could be.*
>
> *Soon woke the dormouse…"Good Gracious me!"*
> *"Where is my toadstool?" loud he lamented.*
> *And that's how umbrellas first were invented*
>   *—Oliver Herford*

9 The Lower School

If it weren't for the rocks in its bed, the stream would have no song.
—Carl Perkins

THE CHILD FOLLOWS the authority of the adult through their feelings of love for their teacher. Their awe and wonder in relationship to their surroundings helps them to learn to love all things, animate and inanimate. The love of the world must never be lost, and it can be renewed over and over in their ever-evolving development.

Their trust in the authority of the teacher helps them to follow form and not devolve into personal likes and dislikes, as can happen at this age. The newly forming social being of the class also helps to guide the students. The teacher is a role model and his or her actions make an imprint on the child. For the child, there is not a distinction between self and world, so the morality and actions of the teacher forms and guides their way. Children at this age engage their feelings enthusiastically with their lessons and engage their will with what is practical and needs doing. Thinking is developed through memory and the learning of basic writing and arithmetic.

In the lower school years, the child is coming into "form" and looking to the authority of the teacher for guidance. It is the role of the teacher to "hold" the form so that a student has a sense for boundaries and limits. For example, how the students walk to the garden creates a shape and pattern to how they will be able to take up the tasks and direction from the garden teacher. Respect and reverence build healthy social relationships. With the transition from play in the kindergarten to the "lessons" and "work" in the lower school, the student is ready to follow and engage in a new way. Words and sounds, addition and subtraction, handwork and music all have form. The garden lesson now has form as well, with an opening and closing.

First & Second Grades

First Grade: "I Am One with My Class and Look Lovingly to My Teacher for Guidance"

Sitting in desks, having individual school supplies and having a schedule marks a major transition for the first grader. They are moving from imitation to active listening and learning and are motivated by their love for their teacher and their will to do well. This new experience excites them and gives them a challenge to rise to. Because of the structure and rhythm of the schedule, they don't move in and out of activities freely, but move together as a class. They also begin to see how their actions affect the whole class.

Connecting With the Classroom Curriculum

First graders are still engaged in nature through the imagination, but can be brought into meaningful tasks through song and story. In the classroom, the learning of sounds and numbers is taught through imagination and mental pictures. Stamping and clapping their numbers, seeing the shapes and pictures of letters, keeps them physically engaged in their learning. Form drawing is introduced, a drawing style that incorporates the whole body, and demands focus and concentration. This builds the foundation for letter writing. In the classroom the first grader for the first time sits in a desk. In the garden there is a formed lesson that still leaves time for creativity and imagination.

Social Dynamics

Learning to still one's own impulses and to follow form is a big transition at this juncture for the first grader. While they want to be in formation with their classmates, much like a flock of geese, they can easily veer from the path and need to be realigned by their teacher. In early childhood, instructions were impersonal; in first grade the teacher can begin to speak to individuals. The teacher helps them to care for and listen to each other through modeling and giving examples of the desired behavior. Transitions are a time of challenge and opportunities for building form and rhythm.

Second Grade: "Awakening from Dreaminess to Focus on Work"

The children's awareness of polarities and contrasts now allows them to experience nature personally rather than being one with everything around them. As they develop their relationship with nature through observation, they can see more of what is at work behind the manifestation of the plant world. Our role is to help the children keep their connectedness by showing interest, care, and attention. Their ability to work within a formed lesson continues to increase.

Connecting With the Classroom Curriculum

In class two, the children continue learning language, numbers, and letters and deepen their skills with recorder, knitting and movement. Contrasts and polarities become a way to navigate and explore their evolving sensitivities both in their environment and in the class dynamics. Legends, stories of saints, and fables supply the context to illustrate these archetypal struggles, helping students to develop their moral sense and giving examples of how to do good in the world. Legends show the human being in conflict with good and evil. These stories indirectly teach the moral values of kindness, truthfulness, and compassion. Animal stories show exaggerated one-sided characteristics in a particular animal that can easily be out of balance in the human if not given proper attention. Observing animals on the farm supports the message of classroom stories. We see the greedy pig, the cunning fox, and the timid sheep of the fables in very real farm animals.

Social Dynamics

The stories and images used by the teacher give children strength and morality in their social relationships. The second grader is gaining confidence and a sense of belonging within the class. The form that they gained in first grade gives rise to focused learning and interactions between classmates. Their enthusiasm for being together takes the form of intense curiosity and interest in each other. Boys and girls play together and exclusivity is rare. In the garden they are adaptable and willing.

FIRST & SECOND GRADE GARDENING CURRICULUM OVERVIEW

Goals:

- Learn to work with a group and complete tasks in the garden
- Develop and maintain a reverence for nature
- Practice patience and kindness with classmates and animals
- Develop a sense of awe and wonder
- Experience the four elements

Key Skills:

- The ability to follow the teacher's lead
- The ability to maintain focus in gardening tasks
- Careful attention in planting large seeds
- The ability to use a trowel and small digging fork to turn soil
- The ability to take care of their tools

Primary Activities for First and Second Grade

In the garden, attention is given to the seasons and their rhythmic changes. Bring this to the children in stories that create vivid imaginative pictures. As the seasons come alive, so will the soul mood of that season come alive in the child. Crunchy leaves in the fall, crisp air, ripening apples, nuts and squash, all assure the child of the transition into the season of fall. Stories and verses can give a picture of this archetypal transition. If first and second grade gardening classes are not long enough for an introductory story, verses, poems or songs can be interspersed as they fit with the work and action of the moment. These are helpful for transitions and bringing the children to experience the nature around them more effortlessly and naturally than giving explanations or instructions. Here are three examples of verses for rain:

> *The earth is wet*
> *The sky is gray*
> *It looks like it may rain all day*
>
> ~·~
>
> *The rain is raining all around,*
> *It falls on field and tree.*
> *It rains on the umbrellas here,*
> *And on the ships at sea.*
>   —*Robert Louis Stevenson*
>
> ~·~
>
> *Pitter-patter goes the rain*
> *Oh, so many hours,*
> *But tho' it keeps us in the house*
> *It's very good for flowers.*

Gratitude is an important aspect of all lessons, as we help the children to see that everything depends on the work of others. The farm and garden are abundant at this time of year and as we gather in the harvest, we give thanks. In our work, we can help nature to thrive. The interweaving of the imaginative picture of each season with one's work in the garden and the gratitude that each season evokes is the true lesson for the first and second grade child.

Walks out in nature help to establish a relationship to the land. Find little special places to be. Walk silently in the woods. Get to know the trees and follow the paths.

With first graders it is good to use the circle as a shape for a garden bed, using a rope to mark the outside. A circle helps them to still see the wholeness of their class and casting seeds towards the center is more appropriate than standing in a line down a garden bed. Their energy is contained by the form, rather than lost in a linear row. Casting our wildflower seeds out into the bed, circle round with a special verse, then water the seeds well and rake soil over the top; in the days to come watch them sprout.

A seed for the Earth,
A seed I sow,
Wonderful wildflowers here shall grow,
Spring is here with warmth and sun,
Digging and sowing, there's work to be done.

In the fall, there are so many tasks that must be done. After removing and saving the seeds, have a sunflower parade with the stalks. Leave some seeds in the garden for the birds. Corn that has dried upon the cob can be shelled with busy fingers. Store for chicken feed, or grind into meal. Helping to build compost piles is important work: rake leaves into piles, load them onto wheelbarrows and deliver to the compost area. Gather plants that have gone to flower or seed and need to go back to the earth such as old lettuce, broccoli, or old bean stalks, and incorporate them into the compost piles.

The biological forces at work in nature are protected through our work and care of the earth, and an imaginative picture leads the way. For example, in the winter, we help "put the garden to bed" by laying a blanket of straw or leaves on the bare soil of the garden beds, to keep the soil warm during the cold winter. The first and second grade children are the ones who take care to save all the seeds for the future after the main harvest.

First and second graders are still playful, yet their hands are more capable of planting seeds. In the spring, creating a trellis for peas or beans is a great beginning to the season. You can also make a teepee out of bamboo or other poles that are tied with twine at the top, then plant a circle of peas or beans. Either harvest them green or plant a variety of bean such as Scarlet Runner Beans that are good to save dry. Planting a "three-sisters" garden with corn, beans, and squash can be accompanied by Native American stories. This traditional planting method utilizes the strengths of each plant to support each other: the corn, planted first, supports the climbing beans, while the winter squash or pumpkins shade the roots.

With first graders, broadcast seeding is appropriate for seeding smaller seeds. This maintains a feeling of working with the whole (throwing seeds into the garden beds) as opposed to separate areas. With second graders, pea and bean seeds are large enough to see and hold and are easy to tuck down into the soil. Seeds such as sunflowers and beets are also large enough to be tucked individually into the ground. Seeds are treasures for us to care for and watch over. As we watch the unfolding of the power within the seed it teaches reverence for the life that is within it.

Other activities such as digging thistles out of the pasture, harvesting carrots and beets, or caring for trees contribute to the work of the farm. Thistles, mallow and other deep-rooted weeds are a healthy challenge for first and second graders. With small sized digging forks and shovels, the children dig until the root gives way and the plant can be pulled out and taken to the compost pile. The children can weed under fruit trees, then harvest worm castings and shallowly work in a thin layer inside the drip line of the tree, and finally top with a thick layer of wood chip, leaf or straw mulch.

Curriculum Examples

YEAR-ROUND PROJECTS

Farm or Nature Walks (Year-Round)

A wonderful first activity for each gardening class for first and second graders is a short walk through the farm, field, garden or other nature area. Stop to taste something straight from the ground or bush, cutting it up on the spot with a paring knife for nibbles. Repeating the same routine each time gives rhythm to the week, seasons, and year. For example, stop to say hello to the big tree, or run down the path to the cow barn, or stop to give an apple to the old horse, or carefully balance on the rocks bordering the flowerbed—each time you walk. Incorporate seasonal variations: in the autumn carefully and quietly walk single file through the tall corn stalks, listening to the rustle of the wind; in the winter, check to see if "Jack Frost" has visited the henhouse roof during the night; in the spring, visit the meadow to see if the "bulb children" have woken up yet.

Fairy Houses & Gardens (Year-Round)

What you will need:

- Natural materials such as pods, moss, bark, stones, sticks, shells, seeds, flowers, twings, mud, yarn, etc.
- A good place to construct the houses such as under a tree, against the back wall of the classroom or other places where they won't be trampled. It's best for them to be in as wild and natural a place as possible
- In urban sites, they can be made in clay pots, filled with soil and taken home

What to do:

- Gather materials in a basket and bring them back to a central place for building (either with the children or on your own)
- The teacher may want to tell an imaginative fairy story to set the mood
- Rather than explaining the project, the teacher can model by putting together some moss with a piece of wood and a seedpod. As the children are drawn to this they imitate and find their own materials. All they have to do is see it and their imaginations go to work

FALL PROJECTS

Leaf Rubbings (Fall)

Find fall leaves and put them between two sheets of paper and rub with beeswax block crayons, watching the patterns magically appear.

Leaf Crowns (Fall)

What you will need:

- Autumn leaves with beautiful colors that are still pliable (not too dry)
- Autumn leaves with stiff, long stems or similar very narrow twigs

What to do:

- To make their own leaf crown each child can select leaves, overlap one third of each leaf and stitch them together using the broken off stem end, or small twigs

Making Dried Apples (Fall)

What you will need:

- Apples
- Apple-corer-peeler-slicer hand crank machine
- Small paring knives
- A way to dry the apples: a food dehydrator; double screens and saw horses for drying outside; cookie sheets and an oven on the lowest setting; or a needle and twine to string the apple rings up in the classroom to dry

What to do:

- Wash the apples
- Set up one or more stations with the apple corer-peeler-slicer and after attaching the apple, have the children crank the apple through the mechanism
- Remove the apple and have the children slice through one side of the apple to separate the rings
- Carefully arrange the rings on the dehydrator rack or baking sheet so they are not overlapping
- Dry according to whichever method you are using
- If stringing, you must knot the twine between pieces so they remain separate and have good air flow
- Store in air tight containers

SPRING PROJECTS

Making Calendula Salve (Spring)

Calendula is a magical healing flower, whose petals are used in salve making. The salve is good for all cuts, burns, and scrapes and it has the golden color of the calendula flower.

What you will need:

- Olive, almond, apricot or avocado oil

- Fresh calendula petals
- Vitamin E oil
- Beeswax
- A large jar (half-gallon mason jar)
- Small jars for the salve

What to do:
- Gather the fresh flowers and infuse them in the oil in the large jar. Use 3 ounces of fresh petals to 1 cup of oil (if using dried petals, use 1 ½ ounces per cup of oil)
- Shake once a day for two weeks
- Strain out the petals and warm the oil over a low flame. Add the grated beeswax (1½ ounce per cup of oil). Remove from heat once it has melted (do not simmer). Add ⅛ teaspoon of vitamin E oil per cup of oil as a preservative
- Test consistency by taking out a small amount and letting it air cool or place in the refrigerator. If the consistency is too hard, add more oil. If the consistency is too soft, add more beeswax
- Pour into small jars and label

Third Grade: "Leaving Oneness to Become An Individual"

The third grader is falling from Eden and landing here on earth. They have matured to the point where they are ready to perform real work. As they begin to notice themselves as separate from the world, they also notice all the contributions that are made on their behalf. Their clothes, shoes, house, and food have come to them by the work of others and they have a blossoming need to understand and participate in all of these processes. These activities are the root of the third grade curriculum. As they move deeper into the real work of the farm, they take on more responsibility and make their own contributions. Growing, harvesting, and cooking food is a cycle that they participate in throughout the year. It gives them a sense of truly arriving here on earth.

Connecting With The Classroom Curriculum

In the classroom, the curriculum is helping them to find a sense of security and a way of surviving in the world which counters the feelings of separateness and aloneness that come with the nine-year change. The third grade main lesson is filled with practical activities such as house building, farming, processing fibers for clothes-making, cooking, practical math and measurement. These basic skills give a foundation for the independence that they need at this time. Bread—the staff of life—is baked from wheat that the children have grown in the garden. Traditionally, the third grade class takes a field trip to a working farm and spends a week engaging in the work alongside the farmer. The demands of a farm are very real, and working with animals, harvesting crops, and doing field-work is an experience no child will ever forget. There are a number of biodynamic farms that are set up to host these kinds of trips and support the practical activities through farm work.

Stories in the third grade classroom go back to the time of creation and give a picture of the beginnings of all of the kingdoms of nature on earth. As human beings became more conscious, a need for guidelines for moral and social conduct became necessary. As the third grader becomes more conscious of "self," the creation stories, or their biblical interpretations, give them a sense of the original moral conduct of people at that time. As they become more at home in their hands-on learning, they build social responsibility and confidence. The moral results of their actions can be seen immediately.

Social Dynamics

Because of the new sense of separation of the third grader, the unity of the class that was so strong in first and second grade meets a strong challenge. The teacher must now find new forms that unite the students while giving room for strong individualism. Farming is an activity that unites the class in their will to work for the whole and not just the self. Here is a place where the lesson comes from the work itself and doesn't have to be spoken, if only to say, "That's not your potato, that's everyone's potato, so add it to the wheelbarrow." Class plays also demand cooperative work and an awareness of the other. Service work and festivals give them a place to shine individually as well as working together as a class.

The third grader has a lot of physical energy, and they want to be doers. Given the opportunity their enthusiasm can be empowering. If not given physical outlets their energy can lead to social conflict. Give them the tool and the direction and they are ready to move forward without hesitation.

THIRD GRADE GARDENING CURRICULUM OVERVIEW

Goals:

- To develop the confidence and skills to provide for their own survival
- To gain an appreciation for the interdependence of self and the world
- To be able to work together as a group
- To unite strong wills with tools and work

Key Skills:

- The manual dexterity to plant individual seeds (larger seeds such as beans, peas, corn, and squash)
- The ability to recognize their own personal space in relationship to their work
- The ability to focus over a period of time on a task that demands concentration and follow-through
- The ability to follow directions and be responsible for a task
- The ability to lift heavy vegetables (pumpkins and squash) and push wheelbarrows that aren't filled to capacity
- The ability to use hand tools (trowels, dibbers, measuring sticks, etc.)
- The ability to contribute to the group and the community

Primary Activities for Third Grade

Because the third grade classroom is so tied to the gardening curriculum, there's a linking between the gardening activities and the songs, stories, and verses that can be used together for a lesson plan, both with the class teacher and the music teacher. Stories and songs help establish the unity and enthusiasm that is so important for the third grade farming curriculum. Cross-culturally, farming songs have been an integral part of agrarian life. Teach the students a song at the beginning of class and then sing it during certain work projects. For example, *The Potato Song* while digging potatoes, *The Mill Song* while grinding wheat, *The Orchard Song* while picking apples.

Cooking is an integral part of the third grade gardening curriculum. In addition to baking bread from wheat grown on the farm, the following cooking projects are wonderful for third grade and link with some of the planting and harvesting activities listed in the next section:

- Cucumber pickles
- Berry jam
- Pan fried onion rings
- Potato salad, French fries, and latkes (pan fried)
- Applesauce, apple pie, and apple crisp
- Hand ground tortillas with fresh tomato salsa, corn muffins (see p. 127 for how to process the corn kernels)
- Pumpkin pie and stuffing
- Stone soup with crackers (read the story *Stone Soup*)
- Fruit cake and Christmas cookies

WHEAT

In the garden, the third grade year follows the seasons. We begin the year with all of the processes of the wheat: winnowing, threshing, grinding and baking, as well as planting wheat for next year's crop. Starting in the fall, and spanning the whole school year, the third graders follow the cycle of the grain from seed to bread. Thankfully, last year's third grade has grown wheat to thresh and winnow in September, and in the fall the class sows the wheat for next year's third grade. Last year's wheat is ground into flour, made into bread, and baked in the oven. When the sprouted wheat plants are large enough, transplant them into the garden. In June, when the wheat forms heads holding new seeds and is tall and ripe, cut and bundle it into sheaves. Tie the bundles of grain tight and hang them up to dry for the summer. Whether your wheat is grown in field or in a small planter box, or is supplemented by store bought grain, this activity exposes the students to a primal activity that is basic to our survival.

FALL CROPS

Third graders harvest many fall crops (squash, potatoes, cucumbers, popcorn, onions) which can be used in cooking projects. The class gathers apples and makes them into apple crisp, applesauce, apple juice and dried apples. If possible, visit a local orchard to acquire a quantity of fruit to process. Before winter comes sow a cover crop over the farm field and harrow it in with a "child-pulled" plough. Smaller garden boxes can be sown with a cover crop that the children harvest and compost or turn into the soil in early spring.

SEEDS & SHEEP SHEARING

In spring start vegetables from seed such as corn, cucumbers, and squash. Plant potatoes, which are first cut into pieces, each potato showing a few eyes. Potatoes require a specific depth and spacing that the third grader is capable of. Watch the sheep being sheared and have the children observe someone spin the wool on the spinning wheel. A local sheep farmer may let you visit in order to be able to see a spring sheep shearing. Coordinate with the handwork or classroom teacher to link this with the fiber arts block.

CORN

Corn was an important staple food for the Native Americans and the settlers who came after them. The study of corn is filled with stories, legends, songs, and activities that come to fruition at Thanksgiving. The experience of walking through the corn can also be a part of your curriculum. The height of the corn creates "wild" magical spaces for children. In order to have this crop available in the fall, plant it in the late spring and grow a dry field corn variety that can be put into storage.

You might want to do research on the indigenous practices in your area, which can yield a rich imaginative picture that can be adapted to create lessons and activities in your garden. For example, in my study of indigenous practices around corn, the pollen was seen as an intermediary between the Gods and humans. It was often sprinkled on the head or put in the mouth to bestow blessing. It was used to invoke and keep peace. The pollen path led to the restoration of harmony and beauty. Verses or songs can be used to reenact our imagination of this indigenous practice. Good sources for practices related to corn include, *Corn Is Maize: The Gift of the Indians* and *The Corn Grows Ripe*.

PROCESSING MILK

The process of making milk into butter, cheese and yogurt are skills that give the third grader a sense of transformation and help them to feel capable. These are basic foods that we consume on a regular basis and now the children have an inner experience of security in knowing how to make milk into a form that will keep over time. If you're able to use milk from a local farm, this deepens the connection and understanding of the participation of the animal, the human, and our food consumption.

Curriculum Examples

FALL PROJECTS

Planting Wheat (September)

The story of "The Little Red Hen" introduces the idea of selflessness in farming, that we don't only want the end result but want to be part of the work that it takes to make something happen. Before the activity, gather the children and tell the story to set the stage for seeding.

What you will need:

- Seedling flats; potting soil; seeds

What to do:

- Create groups: one to fill seedling flats with potting soil; one to plant the seeds and cover with ¼ inch of potting soil; and one group to water the trays

- Seed 3–4 seeds together in each cell or pot of potting soil throughout the tray
- Wheat needs a "family" in order to stand tall later in their life because wheat can "lodge" or fall over. When their roots are intertwined it helps them to stay upright
- Place in a greenhouse or sunny location and water daily
- When wheat sprouts are four to five inches tall, transplant each "family" into a bed or box six inches apart

Story: "The Little Red Hen"

Threshing, Winnowing & Grinding (Fall)

Taking wheat from stalk to seed to flour is an archetypal process that consumes the child's every awareness and brings them to the present moment. Each child finds his or her way into the process and is excited to find a point where their wheat berries are in the bowl with no chaff. Now the berry can be transformed into flour. Begin the lesson with the story below.

What you will need:

- Dried wheat plants; canvas sacks or pillowcases; bowls; flour mill

What to do:

- Form groups for each activity and rotate; If you have one sack for each child they may each thresh their own wheat
- Break off between ten and twenty seed heads from the wheat stalks and place in a sack. When breaking the seed heads there is a place on the stalk called the "neck" that holds the head. If the children grasp at the neck they are less likely to be cut by the sharpness of the chaff
- Close the top of the sack and strike hard against a hard surface such as a picnic bench or tree-stump while singing a song such as the *Reaping Song*
- When all the heads are shattered, the contents of each sack is poured into a bowl
- With the wheat in one bowl, hold it above the second bowl and tip it slowly, letting

it fall into the second bowl while the wind or a fan takes away the chaff

• Pour the winnowed seeds into the mill and turn the handle as the flour collects into a bowl beneath. *The Mill Song* is a good accompaniment for grinding

Songs: "Reaping Song"; "Mill Song"

Story: "The Flail From Heaven" (*Brother's Grimm*)

Baking Bread (Fall)

What you will need:

• Ground wheat flour (if you didn't grow much wheat, supplement with store bought flour or wheat berries); yeast; warm water; salt; oil; baking stone or pans; oven

What to do:

• To bake bread you need an extended period and something to fill the time while the dough is rising. You can combine it with cutting vegetables and making soup during rising time.

One of the most fascinating things for third graders is the magic of the yeast. Let the students watch as you drop the yeast into the warm water with honey that you have prepared in a large bowl. Tell them the story of the yeast eating the sugars and then turning the sugars into gas bubbles that pop up. Wait and watch and finally the yeast will pop to the surface.

Now add some flour. Everyone gets a turn to stir. Then the dough must rise (on top of or in an oven with a pilot light or light bulb, or in a greenhouse). Then add salt, oil, and more flour and incorporate these ingredients well. Everyone can have a turn kneading the large ball of dough. Allow the dough to rise again and then punch out the air. Cut the dough so that each child gets a ball to knead and shape. Then the lovely rolls go into the oven to bake. Eat the bread with soup you have made, or send the bread back to the class after it is finished baking

Story: "The Story of Wheat"

The wheat berry is the fruit of a fully-grown wheat plant and it is also the seed of a new plant. When we grind these berries we get whole wheat flour. The first people collected wild grains and ate them just as they found them. Then they learned to roast grains over a fire or mix them with water to make porridge. Then they made a thicker paste, formed it into cakes and dried them in the sun. These were the first loaves. Then they baked cakes on hot stones. Egypt is generally recognized as the place where leavened bread originated. In Egypt, 5,000 years ago, they fermented batter and formed it into loaves, using yeast that came from porridge that was left out in the open air and accumulated wild yeast. One man learned that he could save seed over winter. He found soil to plant his wheat and stayed nearby to claim his crop. Nomadic people began farming. The seeds of wheat became the seeds of civilization.

Song: "Bread"

Harvesting Onions, Potatoes & Corn (Fall)

Harvesting is a time for seeing the abundance from the work of others and how plants grow over time. Some crops are underground, while others are on the surface, and yet others are in the air. This gives children an opportunity to understand the variety of foods that we eat and how these foods connect with the earth and the human being in terms of the harvest. With harvesting potatoes, children have an inherent sense of wanting to see what's beneath the surface and use their hands to ferret out what's beneath the soil. They get excited when they find a large, beautiful potato. Corn has been in the field for a long time and the children may have walked through the cornrows in anticipation of its later harvest. Corn can be fodder for the animals or food for us to eat.

What you will need: Baskets; buckets; wheelbarrows; carts; digging forks; pruners

What to do:

ONIONS

- Harvest onions and transport to a drying shed or greenhouse
- Snip off the long roots at the bottom and lay them out on tables or screens so the bulbs and tops can dry

- When dry, bag them in mesh bags and hang till needed

POTATOES

- Insert digging forks eight inches from the stem of the plant and pry up to loosen the "family" of potatoes underground
- Reach in and separate the potatoes from the plant
- Feel around to make sure that you've gotten them all
- When dry, store the potatoes in burlap sacks in a cool, dry place until use

CORN

- Pull down the corn ears from the plant and remove the husks
- For field corn, gather when fully dry and hang in mesh bags
- Later, have the children remove the kernels from the cob

WINTER SQUASH

- The farmer or garden teacher should cut the winter squash from the vine a few days ahead of time and leave them to rest in the field
- On harvest day the children gather what they can into buckets and bring them to carts and wheel barrows
- From there, take the squash to a root cellar or shed for storage

Songs: "Traditional Harvest Song"; "Potato Harvest Song"; "Islay Reaper's Song"
Verse: "Indian Children"

Apple Picking, Pressing & Cooking (Fall)

"Harvest Song" *Indian walks,* *Quiet and tall,* *Calls his people one and all.* *Indian walks,* *Quiet and tall,* *Calls his people one and all:*	*"Come my sisters and my brothers,* *At the sounding of the horn.* *Sickles flashing fill your baskets,* *Harvest we the yellow corn.* *Golden shines our father sun,* *Silver shines our sister moon.* *Sickles flashing fill your baskets,* *Reaping in the yellow noon."*

The apple is the perfect food for the younger child. It has a history all the way back to the Garden of Eden and is a very versatile and adaptable fruit. In some regions it's more in abundance than others. The relationship a child develops through the processes of picking and processing apples helps them taste the sweetness of childhood while they move toward developing individuality in the third grade. For years, they have been finding the "star" within the apple and now the "star" becomes a guide for their growth and development. Apples lend themselves to a variety of possibilities for cooking that can be incorporated into your gardening class or the third grade cooking curriculum in the classroom.

Apple Picking (Fall)

What you will need: Find an orchard where you would be welcome to bring a class of children to pick apples; Cardboard boxes; Ladders.

What to do:

- Apple picking necessitates a field trip, which means gathering drivers who will be helpers at the site. It's good to establish rules for safety and respect for other people's property. (An orchard where the fruit is low enough for the children to pick is best. An adult can mount a ladder to shake the tree while the children gather apples from the ground.)
- Have the children work in groups so that they aren't picking randomly or

chaotically. Explaining the method for how to tell if apples are ripe and how to best remove them from the tree is important. We have to be thorough in finding all the ripe apples before moving on to another tree

- Pick as many apples as allowed; windfall apples are really good for apple sauce
- Prior to processing, store your boxes in a cool shed or cellar

Song: "The Great Orchard"

Story: "Oxcart Man"

Pressing Apple Juice (Fall)

What you will need:

- Apple cider press: may be bought or rented from a feed store, brewing supply store or hardware store
- Fresh apples: at least one pound of apples per serving (4–6 apples per child). If you don't have access to affordable bulk apples you may choose to ask each family to bring one serving worth of apples for the juicing

What to do:

- Prior to the work of pressing, tell the story of "Johnny Appleseed" to give a picture of the abundance we receive from apple trees that have been planted for centuries
- Cut up the apples. This is especially important when using ground-fall or gleaned apples so you can see if they are rotten on the inside. Set up cutting boards and knives for the children and demonstrate how to use the knife safely (have the apple sit on end so it doesn't roll, and then cut in half)
- Each child has a turn to toss apples in the hopper, standing a specified distance so hands are never near the hopper. While one child is tossing in apples another is allowed to turn the crank. The apple pulp comes through into the tub below. Children watch while they wait their turn to toss or turn the crank
- Once the tub is full of pulp, place the round cover on the tub and crank down the press-screw assembly to press out the juice into the bottom tray, which will then

run into a bowl. Children can take turns turning the screw. Once it gets very tight add a piece of wood as a lever bar to press all the juice out

- After the juice is pressed, remove the pulp into a wheelbarrow or container and begin another batch
- Pulp is quite acidic and shouldn't be put into the compost in large amounts unless you have enough high carbon materials to mix in. It can be fed to farm animals
- Juice can be drunk immediately or refrigerated or frozen. It is also good served warm or iced and even diluted with water to stretch your quantity

Story: "Johnny Appleseed"

Carving Pumpkins (Fall)

Carving pumpkins is a great activity to have older students assist with, by pairing one eighth grader with one third grader. It helps the older student remember their childhood while the younger student looks up to the older student. The older student can handle the sharper, larger implements. In this way, pumpkin carving becomes a collaborative process and social interaction. Choosing the pumpkin is a magical moment where each child is drawn by their imagination to a different size, shape or color.

What you will need:

- A pumpkin patch that was planted the previous spring, pumpkins bought in bulk from a farmer for a good price, or each child brings a pumpkin from home; if harvesting, clippers to cut the pumpkin off the vine; special pumpkin-carving knives; large kitchen knives (used by adults or older children); scoopers; buckets; bowls; bus tub of soapy water and a towel

What to do:

- Cover the tables with tarps or butcher paper and gather all your materials
- Gather the children near the pumpkins and tell them that they must be able to carry their pumpkin themselves and that they should pick their pumpkin up from the bottom, so that the stem doesn't break
- Bring the pumpkins to tables. The older children or adults should help with cutting

the opening with the larger knives

- The children scoop the pulp out and cut the design as desired with the help of their eighth grade partner. The teacher can organize separating seeds from pulp for later roasting

Story: "The Old Woman and the Red Pumpkin"

Song: "Pumpkin Pie Song"

Sowing Cover Crop on A Ploughed Field (Fall)

What you will need:

- A ploughed or tilled field at least 25 feet square; cover crop seed with a variety of grains and beans; bags with shoulder straps to hold cover crop seed; a long rope

What to do:

- Line the children up along the rope at the edge of the field. The rope gives the children their starting point to make a straight line. As they begin to walk forward, a teacher holds each end of the rope at waist height to keep the line in formation
- Using the verse below, have the children take three steps, one for each word, and broadcast the seed after the third word
- Continue, repeating the verse until the entire area is sown
- The seed must be covered with earth to sprout. One way to do this is listed below

Verse (for sowing cover crop):

Sow the seed	*Swinging wide*
On the ground	*Swinging round*

Harrowing Grain (Fall)

Here the students are doing the work that the farm tractor would be doing. They are pulling a farm implement that covers the seeds with soil. A harrow is a metal triangular shaped tool with tines on the bottom that dig into the soil and look a bit like a caterpillar with hundreds of legs. A chain leads from the harrow to the wooden tree. The students must work like a team of horses leaning against the tree with their weight, pulling the heavy harrow through the soil after the cover crop has been sown.

What you will need:

- An A-frame harrow and a wooden harness for ponies called a "tree" long enough to have four ponies on each side (eight ponies total)

What to do:

Choose eight "ponies" and have them grab the wooden dowel that is part of the tree. When the team is in position, the teacher yells, "Giddy-up!" When they reach the end of the field the teacher yells, "Whoah!" The challenge now is to turn the harrow around to go back in the other direction. Now a new set of "ponies" can be chosen. Continue until everyone has had a turn and you've tired out every child. The seed in the field should be covered.

Verse: "Trot now my pony..."

> *Trot now my pony to harrow the grain*
> *Cover the seeds now before it doth rain*

Gathering & Cracking Walnuts (Fall or Winter)

In this activity we teach the children how to cleanly separate the two halves of the walnut shell. This is challenging and doesn't always work but gives them something to strive for. Discerning between what is the nut and what is the inedible part is an opportunity to focus deeply and keenly on their work. This makes it possible to later eat just the nut without bits of shell and fiber. Nuts are saved for further cooking projects or snack times. This activity gives children deep satisfaction, giving them an opportunity to take part in making food edible.

What you will need:

- Nut crackers; bowls; walnuts

What to do:

- Assuming that you have a walnut (or other nut) tree, start to gather nuts as soon as they fall from the tree.
- With walnuts, they will have wet brown husks attached. These must be given time to dry and fall away. Once husks have fallen away or dried completely, put them on cookie sheets in an oven with a pilot until they've reached the right level of dryness. Now they can be put in an uncovered container in storage prior to use
- Gather the children around a table and give them two bowls, a nutcracker and some walnuts
- Teach them how to put the nutcracker around the seam of the walnut so that they can get two equal halves
- Another challenge is removing the nuts from the shells by hand. It is important to remove all inner fiber dividing the nut and any bits of shell that has cracked off
- When the halves come clean and the nut meat has been picked out, the shells are saved for later boat building

Song: "I Had a Little Nut Tree"

I had a little nut tree,	*Her dress was made of crimson,*
Nothing would it bear,	*Jet black was her hair,*
But a silver nutmeg	*She asked me for my nutmeg*
And a golden pear;	*And my golden pear.*
The King of Spain's daughter	*I said, "So fair a princess*
Came to visit me,	*Never did I see,*
And all for the sake	*I'll give you all the fruit*
Of my little nut tree.	*From my little nut tree.*

Other Fall Poems:

Tall trees in the forest	
Pine cones on the ground.	*Now the Autumn winds do blow*
Tall trees in the forest	*Trees are bending to and fro*
Fall leaves all around.	*This way, that way, so they go.*
~	~

Winter Projects

Making Butter (Winter)

Making butter, which requires a transformation of substance from one form to another, is a representation of the child's inner transformation. Participating in this activity elicits excitement about change and the child's active role in it.

What you will need:

- Heavy whipping cream; pint mason jars; bowls; butter mold (optional)

What to do:

- Have children sit in a circle or at a picnic table, each with a jar
- The teacher pours ½ pint of cream into each jar and lids are screwed on
- The children shake the cream until it starts to thicken. Let the jars rest for one minute. Then shake it very, very fast until the whey falls out of the butter
- There is a lot of activity and questioning around the content transforming in their jar as the fat separates from the buttermilk
- Each child spoons their butter lump into a bowl and presses out more buttermilk using a spoon.
- The buttermilk is collected in a jar and children can taste it. It can be used for cooking
- If desired, mold the butter in a butter mold
- If you wish to make cultured butter, add a tablespoon or two of buttermilk to the cream the night before

Verse: "Shake, Butter, Shake"

> *Shake, butter, shake,*
> *Shake, butter, shake,*
> *(Child's name) is at the garden gate, waiting for her butter cake.*
> *Shake, butter, shake.*

Dipping Beeswax Candles (Winter)

What you will need:

- Slow cooker; coffee can; beeswax; candle wick; sticks

What to do:

- Choose a song or songs appropriate to the season (Advent songs for example)
- Cover the table with a tarp or paper. Place the slow cooker at one end of a table
- Put the can with beeswax into the slow cooker and fill the cooker with water till it reaches ¾ of the way up the sides of the can. Heat until the wax fully melts.
- Give each child a piece of wick. They can either simply dip their wick or tie their wick to a short stick for dipping
- Form a circle around the table and begin singing, slowly walking in a circle
- Each child will dip their wick as they walk by the slow cooker. It's good to demonstrate the action of dipping so they can understand the timing of the dipping
- Ensure that the wick doesn't stay in the wax too long, otherwise the wax will melt off back into the can
- Allow the children to dip their wicks until a candle has formed
- Replenish beeswax as needed as the level drops

Carding Wool and Spinning with a Drop Spindle (Winter)

Spinning is a skill that third graders can do using a drop spindle. If possible, it is also wonderful to give students the opportunity to observe spinning on a spinning wheel. They will be able to take up the skill of spinning on a wheel themselves in seventh through tenth grade.

What you will need:

- Carding combs and sheep's wool fleece

What to do:

- Load one carder with wool, stretching the fibers, placing them from the middle of the carding comb and hanging off the bottom of the comb an equal distance in the air

- Comb the fibers with the other carder, stretching and pulling them into the same orientation until they are transferred to the other comb. Repeat this process until the fibers are smooth
- Starting at one end, roll the matt of wool into a long sausage and remove from the comb
- Place the "sausages," called rolags, into a basket for spinning
- Consult your school's handwork teacher to guide the children in spinning the wool into yarn with drop spindles

Building Bird Houses (Winter)

An indoor project for third graders is to build bird houses. It fits well with the preparation for house building, which is part of the curriculum in the spring. It is also a service project for those creatures of the air that need protection, and a good introduction to carpentry. Research birds in your area and, most importantly, the size opening needed for the particular bird you are hoping to attract (search online for "nest box specifications"). Make sure to check the boxes for habitation in spring.

What you will need:

- Saws; measuring tapes; pencils; hammers; 1" x 6" pine lumber; 6d galvanized finish nails; sandpaper; glue

What to do:

- Cut the following pieces:
  - Three 1" x 6" x 7 ½" pieces for the roof and the bottom
  - Two 1" x 4" x 10" pieces for the front and back
  - One 1" x 1" x 3" perch
  - Two 1" x 6" x 8 ½" pieces for the sides
- Sand all the pieces
- Assemble, beginning with the roof, using wood glue and nails to secure
- Install under building eaves or in trees so they will be ready for spring nesting

SPRING PROJECTS

Planting Potatoes (Spring)

Potatoes tolerate cool weather and can be planted in early spring. Saint Patrick's Day is a good time of year in some parts of the country, and allows us to connect the lesson with the history of the Irish and the potato famine.

What you will need:

- Seed potatoes; hand trowels; compost

What to do:

- Cut your seed potatoes into pieces, each with at least one "eye"
- Set the pieces in a single layer on a tray to dry for a few days or dip the cut ends in wood ashes if you must plant right away (to keep the pieces from rotting)
- Mark out rows
- Dig holes approximately four to six inches deep and one foot apart. Add ¼ cup compost to each hole as you go
- Place a potato piece in each hole with the eye facing up and cover with soil

Story: "Potatoes and The Irish Potato Famine"

The late 1500s saw the introduction of the potato to Ireland. Before this, the Irish had been raising wheat, oats, and barley. The potato, which originated in South America, produced more food and required considerably less work than the grains. Potatoes also required no plowing. By the 1800s poor families ate almost nothing but potatoes, supplemented only by a few vegetables and a small amount of milk. The Irish came to depend on the potato for survival. In 1845, an especially long, wet, and foggy summer caused disease in potato plants and by the fall almost half of the Irish potato crop was destroyed. The people barely lived on what was left. The fungus persisted and destroyed the next year's crop as well. An especially harsh winter in 1846 compounded matters further. It was at this time that many of those who survived started migrating to Canada and the United States.

Sheep Shearing (Spring)

In April or May find a sheep shearer who is good with children, someone who can meet the children through the imagination while being skilled with his or her tools.

Begin the lesson with the story, *Pelle's New Suit* by Elsa Beskow. Then talk with the children about sheep. Explain that the sheep may be nervous, but if we are quiet it will help. Tell them that having their fleece cut does not hurt the sheep, but sometimes they get a nick that heals quickly.

As they watch the activity, the children will be close enough to feel the emotions of the animals and become closer to their experience. Their relationship to the sheep and its wool will be changed.

Seeding and Planting Out Pumpkins, Cucumbers, Squash & Corn (Spring)

These crops have seeds that are easy to sow and there is a good success rate. Because they have harvested and used them in the fall, it is important to plant them in the spring for next year's third grade.

Note: When deciding which varieties of corn to grow, make sure not to plant different varieties near each other or at the same time as corn can easily cross pollinate

Some of the choices for corn are:

- Field corn: for livestock feed
- Sweet corn: eaten fresh
- Popcorn: dried and popped for a snack
- Indian corn: dried for grinding and baking or ornamental
- Flour corn: dried for grinding and baking

What you will need:

- Seeds; potting soil; six packs; trays; wooden marker sticks; trowels; compost

What to do:

- Have the children fill six packs with potting soil and put them in a tray
- Have the children make a hole ½ inch deep in each cell and place one seed
- When all the cells are sown, cover over with potting soil and place a marker stick into the six pack with the name of the vegetable on it
- Place in a greenhouse and water daily

- When the seedlings have made a few sets of true leaves and outdoor temperatures are warm enough they are ready for planting out
- Guide the children to plant in straight rows and cover the roots with soil up to the first leaves. Make a doughnut of soil around the plant to allow water to soak in

Stories: "The Corn Maiden"; "How the Indians Planted Corn"
The oldest grain is corn. When the oak leaves were the size of a mouse's ear, it was planting time. The mother or oldest grandmother of each family kept the fullest ears from last year's harvest. Then the whole family followed in procession to the field outside the village. They all bowed down and offered a prayer to the Great Spirit as they dropped seeds into each row. At harvest time the whole tribe gathered in a great festival. "We seek not the mystery, oh Great One. We bow in gratitude. Be close to us in faith, until the next planting moon, while the gifts of the harvest sustain our bodies."

Making Scarecrows (Spring)

Making scarecrows is an artistic project for the children and something they can see in the garden that they had a part in. It teaches social skills since they must work together.
What you will need:
- Straw; old flannel shirt; jeans; hat; t-shirt; twine
What to do:
- Fill t-shirt with straw to make a roundish head and tie at the neck.
- Tie the hat on the head
- Stuff the flannel shirt and jeans with straw; Tie the ends of sleeves and bottom of jeans with twine to secure the straw; Attach the different pieces together with twine
- Mount on a stick in the garden

Harvesting & Hanging Wheat To Dry (Late Spring)

What you will need:
- Clippers; scissors; twine

What to do:

- Cut the wheat stalks when they are dry and brown, but before they release their seeds. Sing a work song such as the one below
- Two children can work together. One cuts the wheat at the bottom with the clippers while another holds the wheat bundle. The student that used the clippers ties the bundle
- Tie 3 to 4-inch diameter bundles tightly with twine, leaving extra twine for hanging
- Make a loop on the end of the twine on each bundle and hang on nails from the ceiling rafters of a tool shed or other building over the summer

Song: "Islay Reapers Song"
Other Spring Verses: "Birdie in the Tree Top"

> *Birdie in the tree top build a nest.*
> *Fly away, fly away. Take a rest.*

Fourth Grade: "Waking up and Stepping Out"

As the fourth grader gains confidence and begins using their newly forming capacities for thinking, they want both physical and mental challenges. They are seeing the world with new eyes. Finding their place in the world, they begin to see the forces of good and evil, and their archetypal patterns, in stories and life around them. Their awareness of good and evil gives them strength and power, rather than fear and insecurity. The challenges faced during the nine-year change now strengthen their sense of security in their own abilities.

The fourth grade year is the heart of childhood: young, enthusiastic personalities are emerging prior to the influence of puberty. It is a turning point, a time of differentiation between self and the world. Their tool for accessing information is asking questions. They possess a childlike individuality.

Connecting With the Classroom Curriculum

Local geography, local watersheds, and local food sources are important parts of the fourth grade classroom curriculum. In California, this can be a study of the oak and the acorn and how to process acorns into food, like the Native Americans in our area did at one time. These processes help the children find their place, and give them a respect and reverence for nature and her abundant resources. How other cultures lived on the land and what their struggles were is of great interest to them.

In the classroom, the fourth grader is immersed in animal studies, stories, mythology and fables. In the study of fables they can see how each animal has an exaggerated capacity and one-sidedness. This is a lesson to guard against the potential one-sidedness in ourselves. The digestion of animals is studied in the classroom, looking at how many stomachs a cow has and how that is different from a sheep. How does a cow's digestive system help it to produce milk? In the garden, through caring for animals, they can better understand their nature. When the children witness and interact with animals their understanding of classroom stories is broadened by real impressions. The hurried movements of the chickens and the way they take their food and run with it, shows the exaggerated nervousness of their makeup. Seeing the chickens sitting on their eggs, they see a patient mothering which truly explains the concept of nesting.

Social Dynamics

The fourth grader needs to find an individual relationship to his or her work. This alters past relationships with classmates that were based on a sense of unity. Now the development of individuality brings a new dynamic. Geographical studies help them to find a sense of their place in the world, which can help strengthen their role in the community of the classroom. A place must be made for all these new budding individualities.

At this age, they are no longer a "herd," yet they still need to work in harmony with each other. The teacher's role is to harmonize individualities. This implies that the teacher fosters individuality more than they would have in the earlier grades, yet the group's needs must be considered in the balance. The teacher must also keep the lessons challenging. Reason is a newfound capacity.

Fourth Grade Gardening Curriculum Overview

Goals:

- To bring harmony and balance to their new sense of individuality through self-directed activity and independent learning
- To develop confidence in forming their own thoughts
- To develop self-motivation in pursuing their search to understand the world

Key Skills:

- A capacity for both detailed tool use and hard physical work
- Directing tools with intention in challenging situations
- Using pitch forks, rakes and hoes in a responsible way
- Increasing ability to focus with guidance (still distractible)
- Beginning to set goals and make plans that they can meet

Primary Activities for Fourth Grade

If you are able to have animals, the children can take up cleaning the animal housing. For example, the ducks' house needs to be cleaned; the rabbits need combing and feeding; and the chicken coop needs to be cleaned, with fresh straw added to the roost and laying boxes. All the valuable manure that is removed is brought to the compost area, where students learn for the first time to build compost piles in a way that has form and order. It is an ongoing task to transport these manures and watch them transform into valuable humus. You can make an herbal tea blend for the cow that will nourish her while she is lactating. The herbs are picked, dried, and added to her feed.

In urban settings getting to know wild animals that are common to your area gives the child a relationship to these creatures and helps them to get to know their habits.

Wild rabbits, foxes, coyotes, snakes, deer, squirrels, raccoons, owls, porcupines, etc., are unique and have capacities and patterns. How do these creatures work together in the web of life? "Who is the predator, who is the prey," becomes a wonderful activity for the children to participate in. The relationship of wild animals to each other and to their environment is an important study in understanding the web of life.

Fourth grade is a time to begin a study of ecology and our role as land stewards. Questions such as: *How does nature keep our water stored for us? How much water can I take so that others may have their share? What can be recycled?* lead to solutions such as saving water, restoring watersheds, and stopping pollution. When studying forests and trees, we can ask, *How are paper products made?* and *Do we use our forests wisely?* Starting a small nursery of local trees can lead to urban or rural reforesting work.

Creating environments for birds, bees, owls, and beneficial insects in the garden is another important activity. Bees, butterflies, moths, birds, bats, beetles, and flies visit important crops such as fruits, vegetables, seeds, fiber, medicine, and fuel. When they go looking for nectar and pollen, the pollen falls on their bodies and they spread it to the next crop that they visit. This makes reproduction possible for the plants. Bees are the main pollinators for fruits and vegetables. Butterflies are daytime pollinators while moths are nocturnal. Hummingbirds are excellent pollinators, preferring red, tubular flowers. Bats, beetles and flies also fertilize flowers.

Pollinators are in trouble. Their habitats are being destroyed, there are environmental contaminants and they are experiencing diseases. We can help by planting pollinator friendly plants (see page 146 ff. for sixth grade activities). Creating a pollinator hotel or other pollinator habitats helps provide a home for these important creatures. Clean water for pollinators can be made available in shallow dishes or bird baths. Be sure to place sticks at the edges to be used as access ramps by the insects. Dead tree trunks are an ideal place for wood nesting bees and beetles.

Curriculum Examples

Cleaning Out Animal Housing (Year-Round)

Cleaning animal housing helps the children understand the human role in caring for animals, and that animals are a part of our survival. Their bodies become our food and their manures nourish our crops. The skill of lifting bedding material and perceiving the path of travel is an important skill to develop. To learn the value of what we think of as foul is foundational. Children who are able to focus on the work at hand are then able to let go of their discomfort with the smells and taboos of poop.

What you will need:

- Pitch forks; wheelbarrows; fresh atraw or wood chips; rubber boots

What to do:

- Lift soiled bedding with pitchforks and place in wheelbarrows. In using pitchforks the children must have a safe distance from one another
- When full, take the wheelbarrow to the compost pile and place the material neatly on top
- Replace the fouled bedding with fresh straw or wood chips

Making Herbal Tea Blends for Cows and Chickens (Fall)

The children can help the farmer care for the cow and hens through providing herbal tea blends. This is especially beneficial for a lactating cow. Chickens, like humans, can develop colds and can benefit from preventative herbal medicine. Working with the medicinal herbs in the garden gives a sensory experience—as they gather, the children smell, feel, and taste, discerning the differences. This is revisited in the sixth grade and ninth grade in their herbal studies blocks.

What you will need:

- Food dehydrator; pruners and scissors; baskets for collecting; an herb garden

What to do:

- Gather and dry the following herbs (*Note:* if you don't have a medicinal herb garden you can purchase dried herbs from a supplier):
  - ◉ (For the cow mixture) stinging nettle, raspberry leaf, blackberry leaf, fennel seed, caraway seed, peppermint, yarrow flowers, thyme, basil, sage, lemon balm, calendula flowers, marjoram, and savory
  - ◉ (For the chicken mixture) echinacea root, astragulus root, lavender, chamomile, stinging nettle, parsley, peppermint, and garlic
  - ◉ Put the herbs in the dehydrator until dry (up to a few days)
  - ◉ When the herbs are dry, chop or shred as needed and mix together in a gallon jar
  - ◉ During lactation, give the cow a sprinkle of herbs each night in their ration
  - ◉ For the hens, make a tea of the herbs and add to their water each day as a preventative or if they develop respiratory ailments

Story: "Song of the Seven Herbs," by Walking Night Bear

Planting an Oak Nursery (Fall)

What you will need:

- Root trainer nursery pots; potting soil (a less fertile mix); viable acorns

What to do:

- In the fall, give small groups of children five-gallon buckets and take them on an acorn hunt in an oak forest or under oak trees. Look for brown acorns without cracks or holes
- When the buckets are half-filled, bring the acorns back to a table and have the children check for insect holes (a black dot), and discard; also discard any that seem soft or mushy as they are rotten
- Fill the bucket with water and stir. Discard any acorns that float to the surface as these are not viable
- Drain and dry the remaining acorns. Put the acorns in a plastic bag with peat moss

and chill in the refrigerator for 45 days. This process is called stratification and mimics the natural process of freezing in the winter

- After 45 days, some have sprouted. It is fine to plant all, even those without sprouts
- Plant your acorns with the sprout down in root trainer pots
- Keep the pots indoors in a window or in a greenhouse. Keep moist (do not allow to dry out fully)
- Once the trees have sprouted and have some leaves, transfer to a shade house or hardening off table. Your tree seedlings are ready to plant out when they are at least six inches tall and have good root growth

Book: The Man Who Planted Trees by Jean Giono

Winter Projects

Making paper is a strong ecological picture of how we make virgin paper from tree pulp. Do we really want to use trees for a coffee cup?

Paper Making (Winter)

What you will need:

- A blender; old, used, shredded paper; some linters (compressed lint that can be purchased) or lint from your dryer; paper making deckle; large dish tub; felt squares the size of your deckle; rolling pin; dried flower petals and seeds (optional)

What to do:

- Fill the blender about three-quarters full with shredded paper. Cover with water. Add linters
- Blend water and shredded paper to create a slushy mixture. You will learn over time what consistency works best
- Pour the mixture in the tub
- Use deckle to scoop out pulp. Shake a bit to make an even layer of pulp. If using flowers and seeds, add them to the top. Let the excess water drain out of the deckle
- Remove the frame and transfer the mixture onto a piece of wool felt. Roll gently to ease out more water. Let dry

Making Corn Tortillas (Winter)

What you will need:

- Tortilla press(es)
- Plastic bags
- Griddle or cast iron pan
- Oil
- Dry flour corn
- A hand crank meat grinder or food processor
- Lime (mineral)

dried corn

What to do:

- Grow and dry a four corn such as flint or dent corn (Hopi Blue corn is especially good)
- Introduce the different types of flour that are used by different tribes based on their region (for our area in California, this would be the acorn, which can be pressed and made into meal)
- After the corn is dried, take the kernel off the cob (this is a great activity for kindergartners)
- The teacher will need to nixtamalize the corn by cooking the kernels in lime water (lime—the mineral, not the fruit) ahead of time
- For each cup of whole corn use 1 tablespoon of lime (be careful not to touch the lime as it can irritate the skin)
- Mix together in a large pot and bring to a boil
- Simmer for 15–30 minutes (it is done when the skins slip off)
- Let sit for 8–24 hours, then rinse 3 to 5 times, removing the outer skins
- If you are able to have more adult help, make groups that can make tortillas and prepare salsa, refried beans and grated cheese as toppings for the tortillas
- Have one group of children take turns grinding the corn to a fine dough

- Another group can make balls with the dough, and take turns with the tortilla press
- Cook on the griddle or cast iron pan

Making Flower Presses (Winter)

Making flower presses is a good activity for fourth graders as a preparation for their fifth grade botany study. Many flowers are available in the fall and their presses will be ready to go.

What you will need:

- Hand saws
- Clamps
- Hand drills (manual hand drill or ratchet brace) and bits
- Sand paper of various grit sizes and sanding blocks
- Stain and non-toxic clear finish (optional)
- Bolts, washers and wing nuts
- 1" x 8," 10" or 12" boards (pine or a hardwood such as maple, cherry, beech or hickory)
- Corrugated cardboard of a thickness that can be cut with scissors or a paper cutter (at least 4 sheets per press, up to 12 can work depending on the size of your bolts)
- Blotter paper
- Pencils; measuring tapes; speed squares; t-squares; scissors

What to do:

- Decide on the size of your flower press (8 inches to 12 inches square) and have the children measure and cut the pieces. Use clamps to secure the boards to a wood-working bench or table for sawing
- Make a mark ½" to ¾" in from each corner and use manual hand drills to make holes just slightly bigger than the diameter of your bolts (clamp the boards togther for drilling)
- Sand the boards starting with coarse grit paper and ending with fine grit paper
- If you wish, stain and/or seal the wood pieces

- Cut pieces of cardboard to fit the presses, cutting off the corners so they will fit with the bolts in place
- Cut pieces of blotter paper in the same way as you cut the cardboard
- Put the bolts in the bottom piece of wood; sandwich cardboard and blotter paper together for as many layers as you would like in your press; slot the top piece of wood over the bolts; add the washers and wing nuts to screw the press tight

SPRING PROJECTS

Planting Oak Trees (Spring)

Decide whether your site is suitable for planting your seedling oaks as they will get very large. If not, you can have a plant sale, or find a restoration project in your community that needs trees.

What you will need:

- Oak seedlings; shovels; water to water in; stakes; tomato cages; or wire baskets to protect the trees; mulch (optional)

What to do:

- Loosen the soil for each seedling. Oak taproots go quite deep and the smallest oak tree needs the soil to be loosened to a depth of one and a half to two feet. It is quite difficult to judge this visually so you may want to use a measuring device
- When planting, make sure not to bend the taproot. Gently fill in soil around the root
- You may make a ring of mulch to help conserve water around the tree
- Water in the trees fully and if desired, place protection around the trees so they are not stepped on or eaten by wildlife

Story: The Man Who Planted Trees by Jean Giono (retell)

Pollinator Hotels (Spring)

What to do:

- Have the children familiarize themselves with different insects, bees, and butterflies by observing them at different times of day (enlist the support of the class teacher). Have them note what they do, where they land, how long they stay and on which plants or environments

- This will lead to ideas for the students to create their own habitats and pollinator hotels

Fifth Grade: "The Age of Reason Dawns as The Sense-of-Self Grows Stronger"
The fifth grader is beginning to transition from imagination to conceptualization. Greater capacity for memory gives rise to a new understanding of time. The fifth grader is more responsible with schoolwork and is developing an inner compass for right and wrong, which can give them a moral sense of the world.

Connecting With The Classroom Curriculum

In the classroom the fifth grader is introduced to the concept of an ecosystem, and the interrelatedness of life and specific environments. Relationships in nature give a picture of the interactions of living organisms. Their classroom lessons in botany help them to gain a close relationship and deeper knowledge of plants. Drawing plants in the garden from direct observation enhances this study. They are now able to be very specific in their study of nature. This is the time when formal plant classification (genus, species, and family) is introduced in the classroom. Linnaeus is presented as the father of this method. The study of history looks at the cultures and notable individuals of ancient Greece, India, and Egypt. In the garden, plants, foods, and spices connect the students to these time periods and help make the study of that time more tangible.

Social Dynamics

There is a tension in the fifth grader between selfishness and selflessness. The strengthening of the individuality can lead to a critical and even detached attitude. Social and antisocial behavior are at odds, and the teacher will be ever on the alert to guide these changing dynamics with equanimity and calm, as she begins establishing a new relationship with the class. The teacher needs tight reins, a cool disposition and clear consequences. The Greek ideal of beauty and form that tis studied in the classroom can help the students stay buoyant and upright. As the student transitions from the "sense of the whole" to a growing awareness of their individuality, and a new focus on "the parts," the plant world provides an objective example that can nourish their sense of individuality without letting go of the whole. Rather than emphasize individual likes and dislikes, which creates instability in the emotional realm, objective truths observed in nature sustain and support the wholeness of the class and the consideration of others. They are able to relax into the objectivity of nature rather than being forced into the materialism of personal preferences and judgements.

FIFTH GRADE GARDENING CURRICULUM OVERVIEW

Goals:

- To develop a capacity for botanical observation
- To develop a beginning understanding his or her role in caring for the earth's resources

Skills:

- Use pruners to do detailed work
- Be able to identify the node of a plant
- Be able to sit quietly in the garden to do drawing from observation
- Begin general plant identification
- Begin detailed work of seed saving
- Develop discernment through focusing on fine details and parts that make up the whole

Primary Activities for Fifth Grade

In fifth grade the children learn from direct observation of a number of habitats and ecosystems as well as the garden. Each student has a nature journal and goes out exploring, making observations, recordings, and drawings of what they see. Work in the garden entails making useful items from farm products and materials found in nature. The fifth grader is now able to be very specific in their garden work by managing more advanced tools. Drawing plants in the garden from direct observation enhances their classroom study of botany.

Curriculum Examples

The Seasons of a Tree (Year-Round)

What you will need:

- Journals; graphite and colored pencils

What to do:

- Bring the children to an area of the school campus or a park with a number of trees. Have them pick a tree and draw the trunk, bark, canopy, branches, buds and leaves as one whole tree. This will be their tree for the year so they can witness its changes throughout the seasons. Make regular visits to the trees to make a new drawing
- Give students opportunities to give words to their observations.
- This can also be taken into a painting lesson

Plant a Tree (Fall, Winter or Early Spring)

What you will need:

- Trees, either started in your nursery or purchased; shovels; compost; wheelbarrows

What to do:

- Find a location, either on campus or at some other community site, to plant trees. For instructions see *Fruit Tree Planting* in the ninth grade chapter
- Especially good times for planting are the Jewish "New Year of the Trees," Tu Bishvat (15th of Shevat on the Jewish calendar, usually the end of January) or Arbor Day. Arbor Day was first celebrated April 10, 1872. In California, Arbor Day is often

celebrated on March 7, Luther Burbank's* birthday. Highlight with the children how trees enrich our lives by providing beauty, shelter, food, shade, medicine, paper, nuts, and habitat. Trees also absorb carbon dioxide and produce life-giving oxygen

Story: The Giving Tree by Shel Silverstein

Fall Projects

Deadheading Garden Flowers (Fall)

What you will need:

- Pruners; plants in need of deadheading, such as zinnias, cosmos, roses and coreopsis; wheelbarrows or carts

What to do:

- Once the children have an understanding of the growing plant through their prior work in the garden and their botany studies, they are able to take up a task like fall pruning
- During the plant growth cycle, nodes are where leaf, stem and flower production repeat. Students' observational powers are important here since they must find the node and prune directly above it to deadhead the flowers effectively. The purpose of this is to allow the plant to give its energy to the newly forming buds and to stop sending energy to the dying flowers. When leaves are not present, you can find the node where there are horizontal lines at intervals along the stem. This activity is also an opportunity to witness emerging growth stages
- Prunings are collected and composted

Drying Flowers (Fall)

Pressing and drying flowers is a great activity for the early fall when garden flowers are in bloom. As you do this activity, encourage the students to make intimate observations of shapes, textures, lines, curves, colors, etc. This allows them to use their

---

* Luther Burbank, 1849-1946, was a prominent Californian horticulturist and plant breeder who developed over 800 plant strains and varieties, many of which are still popular today.

sense of aesthetics. Flowers, which are diaphanous, open the heart.

What you will need:

- Flower presses or heavy books; flowers

What to do:

- Cut flowers with the students from the garden, being sure to prune the stems appropriately from the plants
- Have the students remove as much of the calyx as possible without the flower falling apart
- Lay flat on the paper and press between cardboard layers of the press or pages of a book
- Once dried, the flowers can be arranged and glued into journals, or be used to make bookmarks or cards.

WINTER PROJECTS

Making Brooms (Winter)

The handle of the broomcorn comes from the forest: a stick is cut, whittled clean, sanded and oiled. The broomcorn is cut from the plants that have been grown the previous season, cleaned of its seeds, and tightly connected to the handle. To prepare the broomcorn the students take butter knives and push the seeds off the tips. The part of the plant that is left becomes the broom head. The whittling, wrapping, and shaping of the broom and handle are all challenges the fifth grader can meet. The teacher's hands help the students' hands as needed. Every household needs a broom. If possible, learn from an experienced broom maker, or make your own prior to working with the children to work out the challenges.

What you will need:

- Broom handles cut from forest branches or dowels; wood saws; whittling knives; oil to remove sap from hands and to oil the handles; broom corn; broom wire (18 ½ gauge); heavy duty hemp twine; small nails (¾" 8d common); carpet needles (optional); broom clamps (optional)

What to do:

- If possible, take the children to the woods to cut handles for their brooms (1 inch to 1 ½ inches diameter and three feet long)
- Whittle the bark from the handles and oil
- In the fall, the children harvest the broomcorn and hang to dry in a shed or greenhouse
- In the winter, scrape off the seeds from the broomcorn with a butter knife
- Attach a minimum 12-inch length of wire to a small nail in the broom handle about eight inches from the base
- Surround the handle base with a layer of broomcorn stalks. Secure the other end of the wire that is attached to the handle to a wall hook, door handle, or table leg to create tension, and wrap at least three times around the corn-covered handle. Turn the bundle, wrapping the wire around it as tightly as possible to bind the stalks securely to the handle
- Add a second layer of stalks and repeat the wire wrap, securing the wire tightly by threading it back through a portion of the stalks
- Optional: to flatten the broom, clamp the broom corn in the clamp and stitch in place using the twine
- In the spring, plant broomcorn for next year's brooms. Start as with regular corn. It will need time in the field to dry before harvesting

FALL OR SPRING PROJECTS

Map and Build A Nature Trail (Fall or Spring)

Fifth grade is a good time to map existing trees and build a nature trail, adding some native plants. Signage with common and Latin names is important. Take the class to the nature area on your campus or take a field trip to a nature preserve where they need trail building. Stand for a few minutes in silence. Then go around the circle and have the students share some observations of their impressions of the space and how they might invite others into it through their planting and trail work. From there, ask for volunteers for each of three groups (the teacher may need to rearrange the groups if any are too lopsided).

Groups:
- Path layers (mark paths with flags)
- Plant researchers & map makers
- Weed removers

The planning process may take a few weeks. The teacher goes from group to group monitoring progress and giving input.

What you will need:
- Shovels; rakes; wheelbarrows; trowels; mulch; flags and plant signs; paper and pencils for map making; native plant books
- Tools for digging and laying the path including mattocks, rakes, hoes, weed barrier, U-shaped irrigation stakes, mallets, level, pruning clippers, and loppers

What to do:

Weed Removers:
- ◎ Remove weeds within the chosen pathway
- ◎ Verify with teacher to confirm prior to removing in case there is a poisonous plant or a native one that looks like a weed
- ◎ Prune existing vegetation as needed
- ◎ Separate woody brush from soft vegetation

Path Layers:
- ◎ Clear the path to be 3 feet wide and level it
- ◎ Lay weed barrier and pound in the irrigation stakes along the edges, 3-feet apart
- ◎ Top with wood chips

Plant Researchers & Map Makers:
- ◎ Work together to map out the plan:

- ◉ Identify and label existing plants
- ◉ Stake locations for new plants with flags
- ◉ Plant the new plants that the teacher has purchased

A culmination of the project can be making an artistic sign that invites people to walk the trail and visit the newly created habitat.

Observing Ecosystems (Fall or Spring)

This is an activity that could either be led by the class teacher or the gardening teacher. Field trips allow the students to observe and experience a variety of ecosystems in your area. If you cannot get there by foot, organize drivers from class parents.

What you will need:

- Observation journals; graphite and colored pencils

What to do:

As you visit one or more ecosystem, help the children observe how each ecosystem, either forest, desert, prairie, wetland or tropical, has a distinct community of plants and animals. Within each system there are producers, consumers, and decomposers, creating an endless cycle or web of life. Observing these relationships in nature, and especially in wild nature, gives the children an understanding of their role in caring for the Earth's resources. As we look at how the forest recycles dead materials and makes a fertile forest floor, how sand at the bottom of a pond cleans and filters water, how all of nature wants to support a growing, living cycle, we can learn to be helpers and take care to do our part.

OBSERVING A FOREST ECOSYSTEM

The soils in forests contain rotted remains of dead plant parts and are usually very dark in color. Trees keep large amounts of organic matter in their trunks in the form of wood and bark. Evergreen trees and conifers are leafy year round while deciduous trees lose their leaves in winter. Dig around under leaves and dead trees. Note what you see. Is there fertility? Sunlight? Moisture? Organisms (micro and macro)?

Observing a Wetland Ecosystem

A wetland consists of water over soil that has little drainage or oxygen. Particular plants grow in the water. Wetlands act as a filter for pollution in water, they help prevent floods and provide food and shelter for plants and animals. Observe water depth, heaviness of soil, water creatures and bird life.

Observing a Prairie or Grassland Ecosystem

The root systems of prairie grasses are an underground ecosystem of roots, rhizomes, insects, worms, and fungi. Observe the variety of grasses, the soil quality and mineral content. Observe the life in the soil and the root mass of the grasses.

Observing a Desert Ecosystem

Deserts are dry and arid with little or no rainfall. Temperatures are very extreme and plants must adapt. Notice these adaptations to the environment in the forms of plants, color or texture of leaves, root systems and soil structure. Observe the soil particles and sizes and shapes of plants.

Observing a Tropical Ecosystem

Rainforests get 100 to 400 inches of rain per year and give life to many plants and animals. What are some unique qualities seen in the rainforest? What are the colors? Light patterns? What is the soil like? Compare the richness of a rainforest to the starkness of a desert.

Winter Projects

Whittling (Winter)

Whittling teaches hand-eye coordination and helps the students to come to terms with the struggle between the inner picture or goal, and the challenges presented by the wood. In the farming curriculum it can lead to making handles for brooms. Introductory projects can include making butter knives or small spoons. As a separate endeavor many schools include a full wood-carving curriculum.

What you will need:

- Softwood (such as Basswood) block (2 x 4 scraps work well); wood carving knives; leather tipped gloves; work benches or tables

What to do:

- Consult a book or other resource to identify an age-appropriate project
- Working outside is great because the shavings can just fall to the ground
- Have enough space between students so they are safe
- The teacher demonstrates proper tool use
- There are two possible directions: finding the object that emerges from the wood or starting with an object in mind
- Communicate the following guidelines to the students:
  - Always use a sharp knife or carving tool (most accidents occur when using dull tools)
  - Be patient and don't rush your work. You can always take off a little more but can't add wood back
  - Try not to carve into the grain—this causes splintering rather than chipping or shaving
  - Cut on an angle into the wood except when marking a line. When cutting down into the wood alternately reverse the angle cuts, like chopping a log
  - Try to use your thumb on the hand holding the tool to steady your hand against the wood. This makes it quite easy to hold the piece you are working on in your hand rather than a vice or clamp
  - Cut small bits at a time, especially when breaking an edge. Shaving rather than cutting will give the best results
  - Work symmetrically, cutting a little on the one side then a little on the other side, checking constantly to see if the two sides are equal

Spring Projects

Observing Monocotyledons and Dicotyledons (Spring)

What you will need:

- Potting soil; plant pots and trays; seeds; plant labels.

What to do:

- Introduce monocotyledons, which are plants that have only one seed leaf (for example, corn) and dicotyledons, which are plants with two seed leaves (such as radishes). A monocotyledon has a fibrous root system rather than a main root. The leaves are blade-like and very parallel. The root and shoot development are separate. The seed stays below the ground. A dicotyledon has two seed leaves and a taproot (a single main root) with many secondary roots. The leaves come in branching pairs from the stem. The root emerges from the seed and pushes downward, the leaves emerge from the seed and push upward, often carrying the seed along.
- In the greenhouse or propagation area, plant corn and bean seeds in pots and watch this story unfold daily to give a real picture of the two. After the students start these plants, they observe them weekly and in four to six weeks are able to plant them out into a bed where they will grow.

Observing the Rose, Apple and Strawberry (Spring)

What you will need:

- Journals; graphite and colored pencils

What to do:

Describe the rose, apple, and strawberry as a family. The rose has an especially beautiful flower and is the mother. The apple, with its strong trunk is the father. The Strawberry, with its tiny tasty fruit is the child. When the bee comes to the rose it finds pollen. From the apple blossom it receives nectar. Have the students draw the apple blossom, the rose and the strawberry blossoms. Count the petals and notice the number of points on the calyx. Open an apple and see the five-pointed star inside.

Observations of blossoms, calyxes and fruits help the students to see developmental processes and stages, from flower to fruit, as well as similarities and differences. Through drawing, the students are able to notice these details.

10 Middle School

We are unlikely to achieve anything close to sustainability in any area unless we work for the broader goal of becoming native in the modern world, and that means becoming native to our places in a coherent community that is in turn embedded in the ecological realities of its surrounding landscape.—Wes Jackson

As the child moves into adolescence there is a certain letting go of their love and trust of authority. Their sense of separation is forcing them to know themselves. Their strengthening individuality and ability to use critical thinking towards observation in the natural world helps them stand apart from the world. In order that thinking not isolate the child, they can be brought back to the world through meaningful work. Given a task and a tool, they can meet the world with an ever increasing understanding of how the world works and their role in it.

Their feeling life, which can be much like a roller coaster ride, goes up and down between the thinking and willing realms. Subjectivity can affect their thinking and feeling. New capacities are available without the needed self-awareness, and awkwardness, outbursts, disruptions, and even isolation are common, yet these only give the outward picture. Inwardly, students at this age are at odds with themselves and need continuous opportunities, challenges, and reassurance. Sexual maturity and the changing social nature of the class further confuse the young person. The curriculum in sixth, seventh, and eight grades is the basis for tuning these developing capacities. Finding the moral middle is the task of the middle school years. Service, a sense for the "other," and self-directed learning keep the ship afloat.

In spite of the fact that authority from the teacher is still in place, there is an element of freedom and responsibility that the student now desires. They want to know for themselves, yet their feeling life is not steady. The curriculum brings them back to objectivity. Teachers now must show themselves to be a part of the larger world and that what they say and do is truthful and real. They have to remain centered, true to the cause, and not reactionary, in order to help the students find the moral middle. The teacher's engagement and immersion in the material that she is teaching must be engaging for the student of this age. To know the "essence" and share it is the teacher's role.

Sixth Grade: "Far from the Glories of Childhood, Riding the Rollercoaster of Change"

The middle school years mark a transition into adolescence. With chaos comes change, and the student does not have an easy time making sense of the physical and emotional changes she or he is experiencing. They are self-conscious around their appearance and their voice can sound vulnerable or be brutally honest. Because the student is ever changing, continuity and form in all lessons is important. Through the chaos, the soul can be born. Through the structure, this birth of self can happen. Their fluctuating emotions will give rise to clear thinking later in the high school years.

In the sixth grade gardening curriculum the student can find a place in the day where the world needs something from them through encounters with nature and engagement with others. It is important that they feel themselves to be an essential part of important work, not just doing things they are told to do. By being engaged with the purpose and design of the work, having some say in how it looks, they invest themselves.

Connecting With The Classroom Curriculum

In the garden, the sixth grader can find the objectivity of nature, while the physical demands of hard work and the rigors of gardening help ground their uncertainties. In the classroom, their capacity for learning is accelerated and they can dive into concepts, gaining knowledge and skills. Gardening lessons need to be detailed, challenging, and physically demanding.

In the classroom, the study of mineralogy is a foundation for the introduction to compost, which is formed naturally in the forests and mountains and ends in the valleys. The relationships of environmental factors such as weather, wind, and storms and their effect on the mineral kingdom are a picture of cause and effect, which is a large part of sixth grade lessons. A study of world history brings a picture of changing cultures and the world becoming modern. When setting up irrigation in our gardens we can trace the movement of water back quite far in history. Roman history is studied in the classroom and in gardening class the history of irrigation in Roman times can be taken up. The way the Romans moved water was an early example of our ability as humans to have power over nature. The viaduct was a key player in the empire and was a forerunner to the way we move water today. Estate gardens, which originated in Europe (predominantly in England) are a model of form and beauty in gardening, which serves as another historical example for the sixth grader in their garden work. Formal plantings of herbs as borders, paths, and plant choices come out of our study of these gardens.

Social Dynamics

Physical and emotional changes affect the social dynamics of the class and often turn it to chaos. Students experiment with how their bodies move in space and try to fit into their rapidly growing skeleton. This same experience happens with their social group. Sometimes they fit and sometimes they do not. And the pain of not fitting is enormous. The teacher is also scrutinized and must remain strong. The storm will pass, but it could take the entire year. Students often do not mean what they say— their words just jump out. Often they act without thinking and only have regrets afterwards. Their capacity for "doing" can be sidetracked by socializing, and they need to be called back by the teacher. The work can call them back as well.

SIXTH GRADE GARDENING CURRICULUM OVERVIEW

Goals:

- Direct students' thinking towards an objective understanding of the world, rather than their ever-changing emotions

- Guide them in forming healthy social relationships that include all individuals rather than a select group
- Encourage excellence in the quality of their work
- Strengthen their interest in and orientation to their surroundings
- Help the students find a healthy balance between gravity and levity

Key Skills:

- Proficiency with use of digging tools (such as spade, digging fork, and shovel)
- Ability to form and shape compost piles with a clear understanding of the elements of which they are composed
- Ability to sow seeds of any size and pot on seedlings
- Ability to do heavy lifting of straw bales
- Proper transplanting of starts into garden beds
- Proper harvesting of vegetables
- Beginning use of wood-splitting tools
- Ability to prepare snacks

Primary Activities for Sixth Grade

The following verse can be used at the beginning of the gardening class and gives the picture of the awe-inspiring magic that we engage in as gardeners. As we work with these pictures we open our imaginations to the realms beyond our sight where nature is at work. With their developing soul life this age group can allow a verse to teach them through metaphor.

> *Invisibly within the seed,*
> *the plant is waiting for its day of birth.*
> *Root, stem and leaf,*
> *the flower and the fruit,*
> *will sprout and bloom and ripen*
>
> *as the sun and rain call them forth.*
> *So Life will call from me*
> *what now is invisibly waiting.*
>
> *—Dorothy Harrar*

Sixth graders care for vegetables and flowers, as well as culinary and medicinal herbs, many of which date back to Roman times. They are called to observe processes around them by paying closer attention to weather, soil, worms, sprouting seeds, and the flowering and fruiting of plants. Keeping journals helps them to find the proper language to do artistic work and keep records, while they move between the academic and the practical. Now they have a responsibility to help plants thrive. The needs of the plant world call for a selflessness that the students are only beginning to embrace.

SEEDING, POTTING ON AND PLANTING OUT

Seeding is a very concentrated activity. Seeds are very different in size from one another. The smaller the seed the less depth it needs when planted, and it takes precision to place only one seed per cell. Looking at the difference between a poppy seed and a pea, a snapdragon seed and a sunflower seed brings attention to the planting depths that each seed will need.

Some seeds go directly into a prepared garden bed and need marker labels. All seeds must be kept in the right conditions of light, warmth and moisture. The teacher must imprint the importance of care and attention, using our growing powers of observation. This takes daily monitoring until plants are ready to be transplanted out or put on a drip irrigation system. Seedlings are vulnerable and teach a certain aspect of care and responsibility.

Transplanting seedlings to larger "six packs," called "potting on," requires sensitivity and demands attention. It also connects the students to each plant, observing the growth it has achieved, and how the roots have developed in relationship to the leaf and stem. The work engages observation and the observation improves the work.

Transplanting out to the garden beds is the next big step. We carefully extract the plant from its cell, flat, or pot, and without touching the roots at all, we open the bed with a trowel, add a bit of compost, and allow the roots to drop into the hole. The hole must be big enough to allow the plant to be planted up to its first leaves on the stem above the roots at soil level without "bunching up the roots." Without that freedom, the plant's future is not at optimal performance. Along with planting, fertilization can be introduced through work with worm composting and green manure ferments such as nettle tea or compost tea.

Watering is now a bigger job, as it takes more water to keep the plants thriving in the garden bed. Students can learn about mulch: material used to keep soil around the plant from being exposed to too much heat that can evaporate much needed water. Mulch can also keep weeds from growing and keep soil cooler. Plants can be mulched with straw, cardboard, newspaper, seaweed, grass clippings, or leaves from plants like comfrey or artichokes.

Along with all the propagation work in the greenhouse, sixth grade is also a good time to introduce the three classes of plants: annuals that live for one season; biennials that live for two seasons; and perennials that can live for many seasons.

Working in the Habitat Garden

In sixth grade the concepts of diversity and interdependence are introduced. A garden is a place where we strive to create habitats for all creatures, great and small. An introduction to the honeybee, mason bee, butterfly, and hummingbird and their roles as pollinators is a first step in choosing what to plant in a habitat garden. Pollinators visit flowers in search of nectar and pollen. They gather pollen on their bodies, and when visiting the next flower, this pollen is deposited. Our food production is very dependent on these visitors. When pollinators thrive, so do we. Keep them in mind and plant special plants that these creatures search for.

A larval plant is where the butterfly lays its eggs so that when the young caterpillars hatch they will have an abundance of the right food source. Monarch butterflies need our help since their population is decreasing. Milkweed is the larval plant for the monarch butterfly. Many wild weeds are larval plants for a variety of butterflies: thistle, fennel, mallow, plantain, dock, nettles, mustard, and monkey flower all provide a home for the eggs and caterpillars. Cultivated larval plants include parsley, dill, and spicebush. For their nectar, butterflies travel to sunflower, *Zinnia*, yarrow, *Aster*,

Ceanothus, Cosmos, Echinacea, lavender, mint, sage, marigold, *Tithonia,* pineapple sage, *Buddleja, Verbena,* and black-eyed Susan. This is just a sampling of nectar plants. There are many more to choose from.

Hummingbirds feed from tubular flowers such as honeysuckle, *Fuchsia,* monkey flower, *Nicotiana,* lupine, *Abutilon,* mallow, and rosemary. Hummingbirds are also attracted to the color red.

Bees love all flowers, especially those of fruits and berries. Honeybees and ground dwelling native bees are important pollinators. Flowers with abundant nectar and visual color such as rosemary, thyme, mint, lemon balm, and all annual herbs in the Lamiaceae family provide abundant nectar for honeybees. Other beneficial insects such as ladybugs need habitat as well. Ladybug nymphs love to live on fennel, yarrow, and many other plants where they feed on soft bodied insects.

The four stages of the butterfly life cycle are: egg, caterpillar, chrysalis, and adult butterfly. They lay the egg, which hatches into a caterpillar, sheds it's skin and spins itself into a chrysalis. The body of the butterfly is formed inside the chrysalis—it is a complete change of state where the caterpillar dissolves and is formed into a completely new structure. Upon emerging, the adult butterfly must warm its new wings and search for nectar-rich flowers to feed on. Sun is necessary for a butterfly garden, and a water feature will provide important hydration for these creatures.

This metamorphosis is also a picture of the adolescent: developing fertility carries the child into adulthood. So much change is occurring. Given the right habitat, encouragement, structure, and nutrients the student will complete their own amazing transformation.

Herbal Studies:

Our animal nature or "astrality" is evident in our ability to sense our environment and move towards and away from what we like or don't like. Animal likes and dislikes come from an instinctual wisdom, while in human beings they can be quite individual and can become too prominent if we are continually swayed by likes and dislikes of a personal nature rather than an objective or healthy instinct. The task of the adolescent is to develop their individuality in a healthy way and temper it with objectivity. In the sixth grade the students' sense of smell and taste can guide them in knowing and recognizing unique and distinct herbal plants. We fed the senses up through fifth grade in order to nourish the body. Now it becomes possible to also to feed and develop the soul through the healthy stimulation of the senses, likes and dislikes. Working with herbs, which evoke a strong personal like or dislike, engages their interest and educates their soul. Taken further, they can use the herbs in cooking, or begin to see plants as helpers in self-care and healing. In this way, the self-consciousness of the sixth grader, the "budding astrality" related to their personal and individual desires and emotions, can find a place to express itself in a healthy way.

Planting an herb garden, labeling the plants, gathering and drying them, and making herbal products, all involves keen senses, interest and purpose. In May, when the chive plants are producing a beautiful purple flower, gather decorative glass bottles, fill them with white vinegar, and drop in eight to ten chive blossoms. In two weeks time, the vinegar is fragrant with an onion smell and has turned a beautiful purple color. This is a lovely gift for Mother's Day. In the fall gather individual herbs, dehydrate them, and make your own tea blends to drink during class and fill tea bags for later use as well. Everyone likes a different kind of tea and they love to compare their opinions and reactions to different tastes over a steaming cup. When given the ability to add a spoonful of honey everything gets better. This introduction to herbs, both medicinal and culinary, will be taken further in the ninth grade.

Curriculum Examples

YEAR-ROUND PROJECTS

Soil and Soil Types (Year-Round)

THE NATURE OF SOIL

What is the nature of soil and what are the processes that form soil? Soil is made as rocks are "weathered" by forces of nature such as rain, the movement of water, winter snows, summer heat and chemical reactions. Particles of rock that begin at the mountaintop are carried over time to the valley floor. Soil is composed of a multitude of ingredients carried to us by these natural processes.

What you will need:

- Large sheets of white drawing paper and colored pencils

What to do:

- Have the students draw a mountain landscape that includes a variety of terrain leading from the high point of the mountain down to forest, shrubs, flowers, and a water element such as a lake, pond, or stream
- Have them change colors to symbolize mineral changes (particle size and movement) as the minerals leave the top of the mountain and transform as they travel down over time, ending ultimately at the bottom of the paper, either on land or in the water
- The drawings become the place where we can focus our discussion on how the earth makes soil naturally over large time scales and distances including the effects of wind, weather, and chemistry

Soil Terms

After building an understanding of the processes that form soil we examine soil types and their composition. An introduction to terminology helps to give a foundation for the practical activities.

- *Tilth*: Refers to the suitability of soil for growing crops. Soil with good tilth has larger soil aggregates made up of particles sticking together, greater pore space that can hold air and water, and good drainage.
- *Structure*: Refers to the size and composition of soil particles and whether they aggregate together into crumbs. Biological life processes help to form a good crumb while a lack of soil biology or compaction decrease soil structure

- *Texture*: Refers to the size of the mineral particles of the soil, from relatively large grains of sand to tiny, dust-like particles of silt to even smaller particles of clay

Soil Terms

Soils are classified into many possible soil textures, all composed of specific combinations of sand, silt and clay:

- *Sandy soil:* Highest in sand content and lowest in clay and silt. This soil has particles that are visible, it is low in available nutrients, easy to work, has a poor water holding capacity and good drainage
- *Clay soil:* Highest in clay content and lowest in sand and silt. This soil has nearly microscopic particles, is high in potentially available nutrients, is hard to work and important not to work when too wet, has good water holding capacity and poor drainage
- *Loam:* Between the extremes of sand, silt and clay, incorporating the positive qualities of each
- *Organic matter content & biological activity:* Organic matter enters the soil naturally through the decomposition of plant litter on the earth. It is moved downward by the action of earthworms. It is also increased through the addition of compost. Where there is organic matter there is life, including microbes, mycelium, and macro-organisms
- *How tilth, structure, texture and organic matter interact:* While soil texture type can't be changed, tilth, structure and the amount of organic matter can be improved through good gardening practices such as increasing organic matter, soil life, and aeration

Shake it Up

What you will need:

- Quart jar with lid for each student, water, and soil sample

What to do:

- Fill the jar ⅔ full with water. Add soil to fill the jar, preferably soil from their home

- Shake the jar vigorously and let it settle for a few days undisturbed
- Observe the layers. Large particles will settle at the bottom (gravel and sand). Next will be silt, then clay, then some suspended organic matter on the top
- Help the students evaluate the proportions of sand, silt and clay to know what type of soil they have (compare to a soil texture pyramid diagram)
- Compare the differing results in each jar. What are the good and bad qualities of each soil type? What can be done to amend it? Sandy soil needs more organic matter, clay soil needs more aeration through double digging, growing cover crops and adding organic matter

Ball it Up

What you will need:

- Plates; misting bottles

What to do:

- Take soil samples (dry) and place them on a plate
- Use a mister to spray the soil until it can be formed into a ball
- Identify clay (a tight ball), gritty sand (won't hold together), or loam (holds together at first, but crumbles at a light touch)

Soil and Water

What you will need:

- Plastic quart-sized water bottles (one for each student); scissors; a variety of soil samples; journals; pencils

What to do:

- Take the plastic water bottle and cut it in half
- Place the top of the bottle upside down into the bottom half. Place the dry soil in the top section of the water container
- Pour an equal amount of water through each sample, timing its passage
- Examine the results. Which soil held the water best? Which soil lost matter and

nutrients into the water? Which soil had more oxygen? How much water was absorbed in each soil sample? Did water sit on top and percolate down?
- Chart the results in journal books

Weather Study:

What you will need:
- A journal book; colored pencils; thermometer; barometer; a weather vane and a sundial (They will need some help with terms and vocabulary.)

What to do:
- Have the students observe the sky, clouds, and wind on a weekly basis, including looking at the temperature and barometric pressure. Draw cloud formations and name the type of clouds. Give the wind a descriptive term
- After they make some notes in their journals, have the students share observations and come to agreement about the state of the weather
- Elaborate these observations with drawings or notes taken from a lesson introduced on the chalkboard
- Do some weather predictions by evaluating the present conditions and imagining what might be coming in the future

Fall Projects

Know Your Tools (Fall)

What you will need:
- Journal books, colored pencils, one of every tool from the tool shed

What to do:
- *"Name this tool, draw it, and tell its proper use."* This happens on the first day of sixth grade garden class. One by one we name each tool, talk about how it is used, and the students draw each tool in their journal book. This is the beginning of stewardship: a responsible gardener knows their tools. Once they draw the spade, shovel, digging fork and pitchfork, ask questions: "Why does a shovel

have a bowl?" "Why is a spade flat?" We notice that a pitchfork has sharp thin tines, while a digging forks' tines are thick and strong. The student can now go from concept to will activity. With this understanding comes a deeper, more truthful engagement with the task and the tool.

Drawing a Compost Pile (Fall)

Healthy soil is full of microorganisms. These bacteria, fungi, worms, sow bugs and many other organisms are busy making our soil richer in nutrients by breaking organic matter down into smaller and smaller particles. We need the help of all of these digesters. Particularly important is the earthworm that ingests soil and organic matter and digests and excretes a fine, crumbly, nutrient rich material, worm castings, which is a valuable ingredient for healthy soil. As our worm population grows, the humus and nutrients in soil increase as well. Our plants transfer these valuable nutrients to us when we eat them.

What you will need:

• Chalkboard and colored chalk; journal books and colored pencils

What to do:

Begin with journal books. In this lesson we start to talk about carbon and nitrogen as ingredients in the compost pile, a kind of "compost lasagna." Draw the layers in different colors on the chalkboard. Students draw this in their journal book, naming each ingredient much like lasagna layers. We alternate layers of carbon (straw, leaves, corn stalks, dead brown plant material) and nitrogen (food scraps, manures, green plant clippings, weeds from the garden). We talk about contrasts between dead and living materials, how the dead materials of carbon mix with the active materials of nitrogen and help balance the one-sidedness of each, creating a perfect environment for decomposition and the accumulation of microorganisms and macro-organism such as worms. This is the foundation for understanding the vital forces within each living thing and how the compost process is transforming once-living plant material into humus or fully decomposed compost.

Building a Compost Pile (Fall)

This is a great lesson that there is no waste in a garden. There is a continual cycle of growing and decomposing, feeding and being fed, life and death. In compost, living things die and then death allows other life to be reborn. Nothing is lost; everything comes back in a different form when we take the time to create the environment. I always get a question, "Is this going to turn into soil?" and I say, "Oh, yes!" When they see the ingredients compared to the finished product it opens them to the possibility of transformation and life coming from death.

The focused attention given to the forming of the pile, where there are definite guidelines rather than freedom of choice, helps the adolescent to find the boundaries of self. They learn that sometimes limitation, rather than freedom, gives strength.

What you will need:

- Pitch forks and shovels; nitrogen-rich plant matter (such as weeds or crop residue); carbon-rich plant matter (such as dry leaves or straw); animal manure with bedding (nitrogen and carbon), if available; hose for moistening the pile between layers

What to do:

- Site your piles in partial or full shade
- Using pitchforks, bring carbon materials to create a base for the pile. This first layer creates the footprint for the pile and needs to have a strong rectangular form, at least four feet by eight feet
- Make a "lasagna," alternating layers of green garden waste with animal manure and carbon-rich materials; layers can be eight to twelve inches thick. Thoroughly moisten each layer as you build it. After each set of layers, add a sprinkle of finished compost
- With each layer use a pitchfork to pull the material out to the edges, forming a tabletop that is flat and level. We do not want a pyramid, as this allows material to roll off the top and onto the ground and becomes too narrow to decompose properly
- Be a stickler about form. Continually ask the students, "Is this a table top?" "Are the sides straight?" "Are the corners at right angles?" "The pile needs forming." The

best practice to make the correct form is to have the students take the pitchfork and put it into the pile vertically facing them, then pull the tool and the pile edges towards themselves. This keeps the sides going up vertically and the top flat

- Moisten dry materials thoroughly. (It will take more water than you think)
- Add a last thick layer of leaves or straw to protect the pile from sun and rain
- Do not add meat or dairy products (they can attract rodents), or eucalyptus or bay (the worms do not like the smell of camphor), or invasive weeds like Bermuda grass
- Let sit for six to nine months

Double Digging (Fall)

Sixth grade is a good time to introduce double digging. This is a method of loosening soil and preparing a bed to a depth of 24 inches. The purpose of double digging is to create a raised bed (not to be confused with a wooden raised box) of loosened soil that allows water, air and warmth to penetrate and for the roots to better receive nutrients. This work challenges their physicality and strengthens their will. It demands focus, concentration and attention to detail and technique.

What you will need:
- Digging forks; digging spades; rakes; stakes and string

What to do:
- Pairs of students are assigned a bed that is staked out by the teacher ahead of time
- After a demonstration by the teacher, they can begin double digging, each taking a turn at digging a trench, adding compost and loosening the soil.
- For detailed instructions on double digging see *How to Grow More Vegetables* by John Jeavons (see Bibliography).

WINTER OR SPRING PROJECTS

Making Herbal Salts (Winter or Spring)

What you will need:
- A Seribachi (a Japanese grinding bowl, much like a mortar and pestle, but with

grooves in the bowl); dried culinary herbs such as thyme, sage, basil, oregano, rosemary, nettles, lavender, etc.; a sieve or strainer; small glass jars or zip lock bags; salt; labels

What to do:

- Place 1 Tbs. of salt in the Seribachi and add about 1 Tbs. of each herb desired in the blend
- Grind the herbs into the salt with the pestle, going against the grooves in the bowl to break down the herbs
- Sift with the sieve and regrind any pieces that were not fully ground
- Package and label in jars or bags

Spring Projects

Making Soil Mix & Starting Seeds (Spring)

A seed has been held in its protective seed coat, suspended in time. Once it is placed in soil and watered, that seed coat breaks and new life begins. The young plant needs a variety of nutrients that the soil mix has to provide.

What you will need:

- Sifting screens; shovels; five gallon buckets; wheelbarrows; compost; peat moss or coconut coir; perlite; small volcanic rock (the size of perlite); kelp meal; fish meal; worm castings

Recipe:

- One five gallon bucket each of:
  - Peat moss or Coconut Coir
  - Compost
  - Perlite
  - Volcanic rock
- Two cups each of:
  - Kelp meal

- ⊚ Fish meal
- ⊚ Worm castings

What to do:

- Place a large sifting screen over a wheelbarrow or garden cart
- Measure out the ingredients into buckets and have them ready
- Alternate pouring portions of each ingredient onto the sifting screen and gently push through by rubbing against the screen to break up clumps and mix the ingredients together
- Ensure that the storage location for your finished potting soil is covered

Seventh Grade "Self Restraint and Self Motivation as a Key to the Kingdom"

The seventh grader is somewhere between the youthfulness of a sixth grader and the objectivity and self-awareness of the eighth grader. Their soul life is in constant movement and they have little control over their ever-changing physical bodies. They long for confirmation that their awkwardness will not banish them from the social world around them. This can be an uncomfortable time for them, and the garden can be a place to "be themselves" and express themselves in physical work in nature.

Connecting With The Classroom Curriculum

In the classroom, studies of the Age of Exploration, the Renaissance period of art and culture, and the study of mechanics, anatomy and physiology, all meet the students inner and outer journey of self-exploration. Some of the heaviness of the sixth grader shifts into a willingness to go on an adventure, move into new territory, and be freer in their self-expression. Renaissance art was made from color pigments coming from the earth. Artistic creativity can be explored in the garden by making tempera paints. The laws of mechanics can be exemplified in the garden by using certain tools and seeing how they move materials. An interest in tools and mechanics gives them confidence in their ability to impact the world around them.

Social Dynamics

Seventh graders are experiencing great polarities in their social dynamics: they want respect, yet they are critical of others; they want close friends, yet they need a lot of personal space; they want to be seen by others, yet they are incredibly self conscious. A meaningful worldview can evolve out of their classroom study of history and the evolution of the human being. This can help stabilize their shaky foundation. The teacher must stand firmly in the center, appealing to the feeling life and allowing individual expression to flow through art, drama, poetry, creative writing, and music. In the garden one must appeal to their sense of aesthetics and give them opportunities for self-expression and personal choices. Making bouquets in the garden to deliver to lower school classes helps them to unite their care for others with the beauty of nature. All deeds are weighed at the end of the day and the scales must be balanced so that the darkness doesn't outweigh the light or vice versa. They will go through extremes, but should not be left on one side of the polarity. The meeting of inner and outer, darkness and light, beauty and ugliness must balance in the end. Finding the midpoint in the self is the goal.

SEVENTH GRADE GARDENING CURRICULUM OVERVIEW

Goals:

- Engage in challenging work that demands full attention and helps to overcome self-consciousness
- Discover laws that exist in the physical world that bring order to thinking and give a sense of security
- Thinking and feeling become ordered by the working of the will

Key Skills:

- Learn and practice all aspects of market gardening: seed saving, soil building, bed preparation, composting, transplanting, and harvesting
- Ability to market produce and keep records of the economics

- Competent use of all gardening tools
- Knowledge and experience with herb growing and simple seed saving

Primary Activities for Seventh Grade

The greenhouse continues to be a great environment for the seventh grader. Making potting soil mixes and starting seedlings has a focus that demands precision. This was begun in sixth grade and continues into eighth grade.

MARKET GARDENING

In seventh grade the students study business math and develop a plan for starting a business. To give a sense of the real work and economics behind growing vegetables, the students can have their produce go to a farm stand. They are responsible for the harvesting, washing, weighing, and marketing with a goal of raising money that gives credit to their hard work. Students at this age need to see real world practices that give them faith that their teacher is credible and farming has a practical purpose. They want to see that their work fits into the real world. Having a business commodity as a vehicle to interact with the community helps them to rise to a place of self-respect.

Market gardening is a way of laying out a bed so that it is as productive as possible. Beds are laid out to be worked by hand as opposed to tractors, and must be narrow enough to reach the center from either side. This works well in beds that have been double dug in the previous year. Crops are densely planted so as to produce high yields in small spaces and to create a "living mulch" which shades out weeds once the plants grow to size. A market garden is a picture of abundance and this work serves a need in the school community.

Long-handled tools are very appealing, as students can gain a distance, yet stay in contact with the earth. The cultivator, a long-handled tool with a triangular shaped tip, can gently work around the young plants, loosening soil to help the plant receive greater water, air and warmth and also remove small weeds. Newly formed beds need "dressing"—a layer of compost added before planting—to be worked in with a digging fork or krail. The bed then needs shaping with a rake to establish the edges of the beds and level the surface.

With planting, we get down to soil level and either plant seeds directly or plant transplants that have been started in the greenhouse. Planting beds with a single crop allows for ease of harvesting and marketing. Root vegetables are seeded in rows six inches apart throughout the bed and thinned later. When transplanting seedlings I tell the students to imagine the number five die-face pattern, and in that way plant in staggered rows, allowing the same space between all plants. This maximizes yields.

The harvest and preparation for selling builds a rhythm with their work and a sense of purpose in the greater world. Harvesting encompasses washing, displaying, bagging and pricing. Start a farm stand where parents buy the vegetables, fruits and flowers. This can bring in money to support the farm, a seventh grade trip, or donation for the homeless, teaching the business/economic aspect behind farming.

It is important to grow a variety of flowers, not just for the beneficial insects, butterflies and bees, but also for making bouquets for the class teachers and for sale. This activity brings back lessons from the fifth grade: cutting at the node and observing and selecting flowers that are in bloom and at their peak. Varieties of flowers that are good in bouquets include zinnias, cosmos, coreopsis, snapdragons, straw flowers, dahlias, bachelor buttons, sunflowers, black eyed Susan, sweet Williams, stocks, *Scabiosa*, etc.

Curriculum Examples

Year-Round Projects

Making Tempera Paint (Year-Round)

What you will need:

- Colored rocks or mineral soil (not topsoil) from a variety of places; hammers; tarp and/or feed sacks; mortar and pestles; dust masks; goggles; fine sieve; bowls; eggs; olive oil; small jars with lids

What to do:

- Assign students to bring sample rocks from home, looking for a variety of colors
- Separate rocks by color. Place each in its own feed sack or on a tarp and cover with a cloth, then hammer into small pieces
- Grind small pieces into a fine powder in the mortar and pestle, using the sieve to remove larger pieces for continued work
- Place each finely ground pigment in a separate bowl
- Break an egg carefully, separating the yolk from the white and saving the half shells
- Measure a half-shell of oil and a half-shell of distilled water and mix with the yolk
- Mix egg yolk mixture with each pigment to your desired consistency
- The paint will keep refrigerated for two to three days

FALL PROJECTS

Food Processing (Fall)

Food processing such as dehydrating fruits and vegetables is an engaging task for seventh graders, as they see the value of processing food into a non-perishable product that can be easily transported on backpacking trips or saved for later use. This builds survival skills and gives them confidence and self-reliance in a time of uncertainty.

Another preservation technique is canning. Students must engage with the forces of heat and water with canning, while dehydration is the removal of all excess water. This fits within their chemistry block and looks at the transformation of substances and many of the ways that heat changes our food.

Fermentation is another ancient and cross-cultural food preservation process that uses bacteria to transform and preserve food. In their study of anatomy and physiology they look at the digestive system. Teaching about fermented foods educates them about the symbiotic relationship between human digestive processes and the organisms responsible for fermentation, specifically the lactic bacteria. Food is jarred with salt and water. The brine provides the perfect growth environment for lactic bacteria, which are beneficial to human digestion. Other potentially harmful bacteria are outcompeted as the lactic bacteria create an acidic environment in which they can't survive.

Dehydration (Fall)

What you will need:

- A food dehydrator; knives; cutting boards; labels; jars; markers

What to do:

- Take seasonal vegetables such as tomatoes, green beans, corn, carrots, peppers, etc. and cut or separate into pieces that are a uniform thickness
- Place the pieces in a single layer on the screen and dehydrate
- When dry, package individually or put together in combinations to make a meal or a recipe. Recipe ideas: for backpacking trips create packets with dried beans for soups or with rice for rice dishes; sun-dried tomatoes can be reconstituted for pasta sauces
- Label with the ingredients and directions on how to reconstitute

Canning (Fall)

What you will need:

- Glass canning jars with new lids and rings; tongs; funnel; towels; labels; markers; timer; canning pot; cooking pots; cutting boards; recipe

What to do:

- Hot water bath processing time and temperature are important for food safety. The USDA canning website is a great source for food safe recipes
- We have had good luck with apple sauce, salsa, tomato sauce, dilly beans, pickles, strawberry jam and elderberry syrup

Fermentation (Sauerkraut) (Fall)

What you will need:

- Large bowls; cabbages; a clay sauerkraut crock or gallon canning jars; airlock lids (optional); salt; knives and cutting boards

What to do:
- Slice cabbage thinly
- Put a one inch layer of cabbage in the bottom of the crock and sprinkle lightly with salt
- Pound gently with a wooden pestle to break down the cells of the cabbage so that the salt begins to pull the water out, thus creating the juices and the fermentation
- Continue until the crock is full
- If using a glass jar, pound the cabbage in a stainless steel bowl prior to filling the jar
- Cover with a round wooden lid that fits inside the crock with a weight on top so that the cabbage remains submerged as it continues to break down. If using glass jars, use airlock lids instead for best results
- Store in a cool dry place
- If any mold forms on top scrape it off and throw it away. Your product is not ruined
- The kraut will be done in four to six weeks depending on the air temperature. Leaving it longer will make it more sour
- If using a larger crock or jar, distribute the finished kraut into jars and store in the refrigerator

WINTER PROJECTS

Winter projects for the seventh grader can include planting bare-root berries and fruit trees, construction projects such as building garden boxes, making toolboxes, and handwork projects such as spinning. Many of these projects take precise hand-eye coordination and building requires appreciation and use of math skills. With seventh graders it is better to go into depth with a project over time than to try to do many smaller projects. For example, making garden tool tote boxes can fill an entire gardening block, especially if you have students in the winter.

Berry Planting (Winter)

Care and cultivation of berries are of interest at this age, since of course they love to eat them. Berries must be weeded, pruned, and fertilized each year.

What you will need:

- Raspberry canes; blueberry bushes; strawberry plants; raised beds; flags; shovels; compost; gopher baskets; watering cans; garden beds

What to do:

- Have the students calculate and measure the distances between blueberry bushes and mark with flags
- Students should dig a large hole the size of a five gallon bucket and as deep as the root ball; if using a gopher basket install at this point
- Partially fill the hole with a mixture of soil and compost, and an acidic fertilizer such as peat moss, coffee grounds, or azalea fertilizer
- Place the plant in the hole and backfill with remaining soil and/or compost
- Water in the plants
- Raspberries also like acidic soil but canes have a smaller root system and can be planted with a hand trowel. Add compost and water
- Strawberries have a shallow root system and can be planted in the number five die-face pattern. Firm in with compost and water
- All of the above benefit from mulch and a drip system. Blueberries may need bird netting at fruiting time

Spinning (Winter)

If one has access to wool, spinning is a perfect winter activity for seventh grade. As they learn to use the spinning wheel, students meet the technical challenge of managing feet, hands, and fingers. This introduces them to the process of taking raw wool from the sheep, carding and spinning it and finally producing yarn that can be made into a hat or scarf. Learning to spin helps them to achieve balance, as they must constantly discern speed and tension simultaneously.

What you will need:

- Sheep's fleece; Spinning wheel; Carding combs

What to do:

It is helpful to begin by having each student create a drawing of the spinning wheel and label all of its parts. Some of the history of spinning can be discussed: its origin dates back to 10,000 to 15,000 BC; spinning was once as common a task as sweeping the floor, etc. Then we take up our wool, directly from the sheep that were sheared in the previous year, and "charge" our carding combs with the wool. This is a way of pulling the fibers into the teeth of the carding combs so that we can straighten the wool. Carding opens, separates, and straightens the fibers to make spinning them easier. When the wool is properly carded it is rolled off the carding combs into "rolags," or cigar-shaped sausages of clean, fine wool, ready to be spun.

Spinning takes time to learn. It demands a strong focus and an ability to keep the wheel turning in the right direction while feeding in the carded wool, holding the tension between the taking up of the wool and the giving in of the wool. The seventh grader stands in this mid-point between giving and taking. Students must learn spinning from someone who is already an avid spinner which my not be you. Consult a handwork teacher, parent or someone in the community, or learn to spin prior to teaching.

Eighth Grade "CHILDHOOD IN FULL BLOSSOM; EMANCIPATION YIELDS CONFIDENCE"

For the eighth grader, the completion of lower school signals an arrival at a new beginning and a task completed. Insecurity has transformed into service and compassion. Self-confidence has returned and students are willing to show their strengths. Challenging projects like gardening, basket weaving, and woodworking call for the unity of thinking, feeling and willing.

Connecting With the Classroom Curriculum

The eighth grade studies of the Industrial Revolution, transformation of substances through chemistry, and revolutionary movements of the past, all point to change and transformation. It is a fiery force of activity that brings this change about. The study of biographies of people who have spoken out and worked for their ideals becomes an appropriate lesson at this stage of their development. The eighth grader must consider that they are a world shaper as well. They too can rise to take up a task and make a contribution.

Verse for the Beginning of Class:

> *A vision without a task is but a dream.*
> *A task without a vision is but a drudgery.*
> *A vision with a task is the hope of the future.*
> —*From a Church in Sussex, England c.1730*

In the garden, we stress the power of the individual to take up a task and bring it to completion. This same principal applies in cooking, farming, and basket weaving.

Social Dynamics

Eighth graders have a need to feel united as a class and if the groundwork for this has not been laid in previous years it will be a rocky ride. Tools such as non-violent communication and group work in the form of life skills development can be very helpful. Emancipation is necessary, yet the teacher and parent must remain firmly in place, allowing freedom while still holding boundaries. Girls and boys find very different outlets for their feelings at this age. The girls delight in sharing emotions and feelings while boys can be uncommunicative in this realm and appear harsh and closed in their feeling life. An interesting dynamic often takes place in a basket weaving class. Students relax while working with their hands. The weaving creates harmonious brain patterns and an atmosphere of speaking and listening, as well as objectivity and openness in conversation, with both boys and girls speaking and listening to each other. Repetitious artistic activities that require balance, attention, and judgment transform the "astrality" of the teenager.

EIGHTH GRADE GARDENING CURRICULUM OVERVIEW

Goals:

- Reinforce the strength of objective thinking by coming back to the phenomena
- Give space to individuality in order to encourage personal interest and self-initiated learning
- Expect respect and give respect

Key Skills:

- Mastery of market gardening skills
- Independence and leadership in food preparation
- Food production and community service is achieved with students' own enthusiasm
- Capacity for propagation work and plant care that involves significant responsibility and detail

Primary Activities for Eighth Grade

Students continue the preparation of soil mixes requiring measuring and sifting of many separate materials in specific amounts. All aspects of greenhouse work, from seed sowing, germination, propagation, and seed saving are continued. Chemistry is studied through cooking, and health and hygiene are practiced through making body and facial care products.

The eighth grader is now ready to reach out into the world through community service. Their work in the garden can take on the role of harvesting and delivering produce to those in need. Through this they see that there is a world of needs beyond their tight social circle. Going to homeless shelters, serving and cooking food and listening to stories of the homeless men and women fosters a compassion that stimulates their idealism and their wish to make the world a better place. Visiting the elderly, and singing and playing music for them, gives students an opportunity to include and respect elders.

Grounds work on the campus is another service project for eighth graders to take up. Trees need limbing and pruning to remove the old dead wood. Leaves need raking and to be added to compost piles. The school landscape is enhanced with a top dressing of finished compost. Old, dead flowers can be cut back to encourage new growth. When the younger students see the older students working in the "common space" they will want to emulate this kind of responsibility. In order for the eighth graders to be allowed this public task, they must be a proper example.

Eighth graders also need a time for reflection. The garden is a perfect place to sit and observe nature and write poetry or paint pictures with words through creative writing. They will need a prompt in order to stimulate their creativity.

Curriculum Examples

Year-Round Projects

Grounds work (Year-Round)

As the students mature, their focus is less on their own sense of pleasure and more on the wish to do real, purposeful work. They start to see that skill building comes from doing tasks that may not naturally happen in their home life. Hence they gain an appreciation for carpentry and building repair. Visual and structural projects on the school grounds, in the garden, or on the farm meet the eighth grader's need to do work that has immediate results and demands skill. The projects are site specific and can include: painting or building a tool shed, building a gazebo, repairing animal fencing and tending the landscaping around the school. Building projects like arbors or benches for the campus are also great opportunities for the eighth grader to use their skills.

Groups for building should be four to six students at the most. This is a good time to have an assistant, parent helper, or twelfth grader. Safe supervision and use of tools is essential throughout the process. While students are full of enthusiasm and confidence, do not take your eyes off them while using power tools. All decisions regarding design and planning should involve the student group. This can be a time of many opinions and a good process of sorting out the final decision.

Winter Projects

Basket Weaving (Winter)

At a time when the eighth grader is searching for their own identity, the art of basket weaving gives them time for contemplation as well as the opportunity to make useful traditional vessels. Basket weaving is a path of self-development. There is an inner and outer space to the basket, hence more awareness of the student's own inner and outer space. The students meet places of difficulty and frustration. As they meet obstacles in their basket weaving they also meet obstacles in their own biography that they must overcome. This is their challenge. While their hands are busy moving and shaping materials that must conform to certain techniques; each basket has its own unique ways of resisting this shaping. The fingers must be adept at sensing this give-and-take, and at the same time, they are sending signals to the brain that the student must be sensitive to in order to make good decisions. In class we call this "finger intelligence." They must be aware of their own inner listening as they make the forms, as well as the aesthetic of colors, patterns and types of materials. With help and advice they find the will to overcome the obstacles because, eventually, either the material conforms or something must be redone. The way to success is perseverance.

There is also the opportunity for socializing while making the basket. Basket weaving creates a wonderful social mood. They come in excited and get right to work. They can't wait to start the next one. There is a certain intimacy that comes with a craft that is so ancient and archetypal. We talk about the indigenous people whose lives depended on their baskets, and the cultural practices that this craft instilled. It is also an opportunity to get to know the usefulness of wild plants that all have a role in our craft.

What you will need:

- Pruners; scissors; water buckets for soaking reeds and a demonstration table where students can learn techniques and see a display of basket examples; store bought basket weaving reeds, both flat and round and of different widths and sizes, wooden embroidery hoops, jute, hemp twine, raffia and yarn; a variety of fresh wild plant materials such as willow (curly and straight), red osier dogwood, grape vines, iris leaves, *Crocosmia* leaves, cattail leaves, cedar bark, English ivy.

What to do:

Eight graders learn the basic parts of a basket, starting with the egg basket—ribs, frame and handle—in order to skillfully and artistically make a small, simple basket. They are introduced to a number of materials, both storebought and gathered from nature. They learn to shape their first basket through the weaving of store bought materials. Once this basket is completed, the students can expand to different styles, shapes, forms and patterns, using more wild gathered materials, which are harder to work with.

Basket weaving can be done outdoors in the fall or in a greenhouse in the winter. It is important to have a place to store a variety of materials. Our basket weaving is done in the winter, in a large greenhouse with a dirt floor. Our materials are gleaned from different places on the campus and the students must cut the materials as they need them so they are fresh and flexible. Throughout the course the students complete three to five baskets. Our first basket is a simple "egg basket" made with reed, yarn, jute, and embroidery hoops. Then we make a larger egg basket from materials that we harvest. Next we make a small twined basket from thin reed and make it again from harvested materials. For those who complete all four, they can choose to make a splint basket (a square woven base with a handle attached) or a pine needle basket.

Alistair Bleifuss

11 High School

THE ABILITY "TO KNOW" through one's thinking needs to inform the ability to "do the right thing." As the adolescent enters high school, thinking, feeling, and willing are not in a fully balanced alignment. What they know with their minds cannot be demonstrated quite yet by their actions, and they don't yet have a steady feeling life to guide either the thinking or the will. There can be moments of extreme maturity and insight and, a moment later, a childlike action that is out of place. The feeling life can be childlike and playful and it can seem that everything that they have learned has been forgotten. With warm-hearted guidance from their teachers and clarity in their lessons, they can begin to align their thoughts and feelings. Humor and clear guidelines with their social behavior and academic requirements give both acceptance and structure. The tendency towards impulsiveness can be balanced with their will "to know."

Physical work and movement are an outlet and a further guide for the student's sense of security in the physical world. The process of discernment and insight has to develop freely over time. The young person needs to find their place between form and freedom, self and the world. Thinking—the ability to abstract—and intellectual development, which was held back in the early years, can flourish and ripen at this age. Feeling and willing, which have been cultivated previously must still be stimulated through our teaching. One-sided intellectualism can lead to materialism, whereas thinking infused with social conscience and empathy gives rise to self-reliance, insight, and a will to do good in the world. In the course of the high school years, it is the ideal that thinking, feeling, and willing are equally essential and engaged in all learning and the development of the student.

The adolescent is physically capable of having an impact on their environment. By combining their will capacities with the healthy development of the feeling realm (reverence for nature and a social feeling) and the thinking realm (seeing the patterns and processes of nature) they can now begin to grasp the world and leave their mark. What empowerment this brings!

Preparing High School Students for a Sustainable Future

The present environmental situation calls us to be conscious participants in healing rather than depleting the earth's resources. High school students need to become ecologically literate, which is to understand the principles of ecology and the language of nature. As they learn the concepts of balanced ecosystems and sustainability, they can begin to ask to what degree our current way of life supports balance and sustainability.

As we move from the concept of ecosystem to the practice of farming we are working with the question, "How can we work with the earth in a sustainable way, while taking resources from the soil to grow our food?" We take a hard look at the industrial model of agriculture, which has had a tremendous impact on the earth both environmentally and socially. Industrial agriculture has clothed itself in many myths and these must be unraveled so that the student can see its environmental impact and make clear choices as a consumer as well as a farmer.

We live in a time where the well-being of the earth and all of humanity are at risk. Every choice we make, from the food we eat, to the lifestyle we live and the resources that we take, affect the ecosystem. Once informed, students can make responsible choices. Although the industrial model may seem quite dark, the biodynamic and organic practices bring hope for the future. These students can bring this hope into the future.

Students are eager to know the complexities of farming so that they can be participants in the solutions. Guided by the teacher, they become full participants in the real work of the farm. They are also guided by their new understanding of the great need for a form of agriculture that is healing to both the human and the earth.

A note on high school gardening activities: Although activities in the following sections are organized according to grade, many of them are applicable to any grade depending on your particular block rotation and what is needed in the garden for that season. This is especially true for the core gardening activities of annual seedling propagation, vegetable bed preparation, planting, harvesting, deadheading, and pruning. It's important to consider the needs of your individual program and the student's ages and how those two fit together. Not everyone has a high school, so middle school students may be filling the niche that is suggested for high school here in terms of the practical needs of the garden. While all grades may be involved with seeding and harvesting, these tasks can be separated into large and small seeds or sturdy and delicate crops for younger and older students.

Ninth Grade: "How do I do it? How do I learn it? How do I make it?"

In the transition to high school the ninth grade student begins a youthful apprenticeship, eager to learn. Their model of learning is to first trust the teacher's presentation, ask questions, and then make the ideas their own. Their skills and experience from previous years provide a foundation. They test the world and must find their own sense of truth. Socially, they have taken a leap from the top of the ladder in middle school, into an unknown pool of the high school community where they must look up again and find their way.

Connecting With the Classroom Curriculum

The themes for ninth grade are the earth as a whole entity in the study of geology and the ability to recognize rocks and name them. We inhabit a diverse planet called Earth. From these topics we build a foundation for ecological principals. With the introduction to farming, the students are asked to reflect and write about their first agricultural experience. When a family farming legacy exists for them, recalling and writing about it makes it more tangible.

The revolutions history block depicts human struggles to uphold ideals. They look for themes that show up in our present world situation and write about the interconnections. In physics, they study mechanics in order to gain an objective view of how energy is used. In the farming ecology block, as we look at industrialization we can explore the true costs of technology. The classroom chemistry block also informs the garden work, while gardening activities exemplify the chemical processes they are learning about. Combustion, decomposition, and distillation are examples of substances transformed through time with heat and pressure.

Social Dynamics

Logic is being born in the ninth grader, while passions and desires create uneven terrain in the classroom and pull at their developing sense of self. The teacher's forming of the class sets a tone for the coming years and it must be done tenderly, yet with strength and compassion. Social inclusion can be fostered by holding class meetings and by taking class trips. Physically challenging work and form are important in the gardening classes. They need support in adjusting to the rigors of high school and to relearn their place and find a balance in a new group.

Ninth Grade Gardening Curriculum Overview

Goals:
- Students begin self-initiated work
- Students strengthen their independence
- Inner activity and their ability to conceptualize becomes evident in their work

Key Skills & Concepts:

- The ability to work with others without loosing focus
- Application of previously learned carpentry skills in garden building projects
- Proficient knowledge and use of tools. Deeper interest in tools is now possible
- Ability to use thinking to solve problems
- Strong foundation in soil science, composting, plant families, herbs, greenhouse work and water catchment
- Begin to understand and apply ecoliteracy

Primary Activities for Ninth Grade

High school students are full of idealism, which can express itself in a true understanding and caring for the earth. It's a great time to introduce environmental issues along with positive solutions. How can we broaden the scope of environmental awareness in the high school student and reach out to our greater community?

Environmental issues become important to the student at this age. Their interest is supported with a good foundation in water ecology, soils science, composting, food production, and an introduction to biodynamic agriculture. They become more informed and responsible for their own well-being. Students in ninth grade want to know how and why things are the way they are and how it all relates to them personally. They work on independent research and gain practical knowledge, which they share with their classmates.

Curriculum Examples

YEAR-ROUND PROJECTS

Journaling (Year-Round)

AGRICULTURAL ROOTS:

Students write about their first agricultural experience. Some remember a field trip to a farm; while for others, it is gardening with their mother. Recalling how they first met agriculture helps them gather together all of the threads that have come from those experiences to bring them to where they are now. Next is a time of sharing these memories and finding interest in each other's experiences, bringing insight into how our elders or our life experiences have introduced us to the land.

Sense of Place:

A second writing activity is looking at landscapes. Students think back to a special place where they went when they were younger, describing the land in as much detail as possible. How did the elements of the land affect their daily activity? What were the sounds, the trees, the hills, and the neighborhood culture? What was their "sense of place"? Where do they belong today? All of these questions help the students to discover their own personal relationship to the landscape.

Energy:

To understand our place on earth we look at how our energy is produced and delivered to us. Is it nuclear, geothermal, solar, or coal? What are the appliances in our homes that use the most energy? How are our homes heated? How do we transport ourselves to school?

Water:

Water is an integral aspect of our daily lives and landscapes. How do we get the water that is in our homes? Is it from a well or from municipal water service? What is rainwater catchment? As a practical activity in the garden, we build berms and swales (trenches and hills) to move water safely and slowly through the garden.

Land:

A study of geology deepens the students' sense of place. What makes soil? What are the types of rock forming the grounds at our school, at our homes, in the wild areas? The soil that we inhabit is the geology of the place that we are going to be farming. Understanding our use of resources to grow food leads to more awareness in our agriculture practices.

FALL PROJECTS

Herbal Studies (Fall)

In the fall, ninth graders have a six-week intensive block, taking up the study of the culinary and medicinal properties of herbs. This course fits in developmentally, as they are seeing their changing bodies and the ways in which they can be empowered to care for themselves. This can take the form of making herbal teas, medicines, culinary dishes, and even herbal cosmetics. The question, "What does the plant have to teach me and how can I learn more about it?" deepens their own understanding of themselves. The plant world can also mirror our own soul moods, support us in illness and nourish our bodies with healing foods.

This course has four components: research, practical work, drawing, and a final project. There are many books available at the library and it could also be very useful to build your own library as a teacher. Each student chooses three herbs to study and spends time researching their culinary and medicinal properties, finding a myth or story, and a recipe. In their notebooks they describe the plant physically and create a color drawing. An introduction to the Latin names of herbs is very important. They must know how to find genus, species, and family for each of their three herbs. During this course the students also go out and harvest their herbs in the garden. They process their herbs in many different ways: sometimes in a food dryer, sometimes infused in oil, sometimes roasted and ground into a powder. These processes deepen the students' knowledge and relationship to the plants and give them the experience of transformation of materials.

Their final project is a culmination of their practical experience and research and is shared with the rest of the class. Products resulting from these final projects have ranged from dill pickles, lavender lip balm, thyme quiche, rosemary focaccia, mugwort dream pillows, lavender cake, rose cupcakes, stinging nettle tea, and basil pesto. The possibilities are unlimited. This is a healthy process of exploration and experimentation and it's fun to make and share the creations with the class.

Making Biodynamic Compost (Fall)

Through a discussion of compost we review how essential it is to the building of topsoil, how it is our first and most important sustainable farming practice, and how it allows us to grow crops year after year. We now go from the conceptual to the practical by building a compost pile. What was introduced in sixth grade is now replicated in ninth grade. The students now have the thinking capacity to understand the concepts at work in building compost and take responsibility for building the pile with this awareness.

Students use scythes to cut high grass, which is a good nitrogen layer for the pile. Old, wet straw is a good carbon layer. Chopped kale plants and thistles from the field add more nitrogen. The chicken and rabbit manure add nitrogen as well. Straw used as bedding in animal housing adds carbon. We shape and form the pile, like a pan of lasagna. The biodynamic preparations are introduced when we are finished forming the pile. A discussion of the different preparations, from horn manure to horn silica, to the compost preparations introduces the topic. Our herbal studies class has introduced them to many of the plants that are used in the compost preparations, so now they can understand how these herbs can be medicine for the compost, and then for the plants. Many interesting questions arise that give room for further discussion. Two students stir the valerian, while others make the necessary holes in the pile. Each student takes a turn putting a teaspoon of stinging nettle, oak bark, chamomile, dandelion, or yarrow properly into the holes in the pile. Valerian is sprayed on as a protective sheath. When, after a period of time, we observe the pile, the changes in quality, shape, and size of transformed material is startling to the students.

Winter Projects

Fruit-Tree Planting (Winter)

Ninth grade students love to dig! Planting fruit trees necessitates digging holes the size of a five-gallon bucket. Insert a five-gallon size gopher basket into the hole. It is important that the roots have space to spread out. Additional humus is added to the soil that is placed around the tree roots. It is important to keep the soil line the same as it was in the pot and below the graft if it is a bare root tree. The tree needs a stake and plastic chain or twine to support it from wind during its early years.

Planting fruit trees is a great opportunity to introduce the permaculture concept of guilds. A guild of plants has a common interest. They are interdependent and work together for the benefit of the whole. The fruit tree becomes the matriarch of this community of plants, while other plants planted outside the drip line of the fruit tree each bring a different beneficial quality to the guild. For example, there are plants that are beneficial insect attractors, mulch material producers, and nutrient accumulators. By planting fruit trees you are assuring that students will have fruit to eat and trees to prune in the future.

Spring Projects

Seeding (Spring)

In January of the previous year when you make your crop plan, choose the crops and varieties that fit your need and climate. Based on your crop plan, create a greenhouse-seeding plan that the students can work from. In the spring the students mix potting soil, fill flats and sow seeds. While getting prepared for this activity it is important to give students a picture of the "potential energy" that lives within the seed coat and the conditions of water, warmth, light and nutrients that must be present for the seed to sprout and grow. With seeding it is important for the students to know that the size of the seed determines the depth of its planting. Sowing celery or poppy seeds is much more challenging than sowing beet or sunflower seeds. Following germination and the development of a few sets of true leaves the students proceed to the work of transplanting and finally planting out in the garden. Other seeds need to be planted directly into the garden beds that have been properly prepared. Size of seed, depth, and spacing are important with direct sowing.

Tenth Grade "How Do We Know What We Know?"

The student in the tenth grade is seeking not only information, but insights. They need to know the origin of things and how it all came to be. Existentialism is a real experience for them at this age, and they do not have all the tools at their disposal. They are trying to synthesize all that they know in order to make sense of the world. There is a need to hide while they sort it all out. This experience is a recapitulation of the nine-year change and they are vulnerable. Comparison becomes a tool to gain understanding. Emotional extremes can be balanced by seeking analytical laws, which lead to the ability to form judgments. Thinking begins to align the emotions.

Connecting With the Classroom Curriculum

In the main lesson a study of the origins of civilization give a sense of how we arrived at this point in time. The story of the Odyssey is a parallel to their own journey into the unknown. Odysseus travels far and wide seeing much of the world, while seeking ultimately to return home safely. In their drama main lesson they perform a Greek play that is a tragedy of transgression, harsh lessons, and violent storms. They learn that when sound powers of judgment are found, the world becomes a better place. In physics, they learn how arches and bridges are able to sustain weight, constructing and testing miniature models. In the garden real bridges are constructed. Students also take up the fine skill of grafting fruit trees. Here they must be precise and follow the rules. If the cut is not accurate the cells will not grow together to accept the scion. When done correctly a powerful tree will be birthed. This is a process that depicts their journey. The scion is the tenth grader, a powerful piece of wood, ready to sprout and bear fruit.

Social Dynamics

At this stage some students hide by forming bonds with a few students who they are most aligned with. They feel greatly challenged inwardly, without the language to speak about it. Sexuality and power are inner forces that they must reckon with. The shadow side wants to take over, yet it needs to be seen as a trickster, not the real self. Hard physical work, both inner and outer, helps the students survive these challenges.

TENTH GRADE GARDENING CURRICULUM OVERVIEW

Goals:

- Student gains the strength to develop sound judgment
- The student finds the inner strength to take on leadership roles
- The student can use their trials as insight, and as a way to refocus their goals and intentions
- Students achieve self-determination

Key Skills:

- Gain an ability to do fruit tree grafting
- Understand and practice permaculture methods
- Hold interest in the natural world and have the confidence to contribute to its well-being
- Develop an ability to be reflective about nature in creative writing and poetry

Primary Activities for Tenth Grade

Now the tenth grader can begin to see herself as an orchardist, taking up the skills of land stewardship and management. Through their studies in permaculture they begin to understand the relationship between wild zones and the frequently trafficked zones of the human being and how they work together. They see their role as garden designers and land stewards working in harmony with nature. Their growing inner maturity helps them to be able to see the interrelatedness between the human being and the land.

Curriculum Examples

YEAR-ROUND PROJECTS

Poetry Through Water Ecology (Year-Round)

"[There] are three interrelated principles: that the word—whether written or spoken—is a living energy, that poetry is an imaginative discipline and that creative writing enhances subtle acts of healing." —Peter Abbs

In the tenth grade, poetry can be a vehicle for learning and applying ecological ideas related to water. In a two-week block, introduce watersheds and local water sources. Each day can begin with reading a water poem. Then, introduce concepts of water through imaginative pictures and poetry. Next, the class generates a "word bank," a list of descriptive words that relate to water. Small group work can then deepen the understanding of these concepts. Each group writes a poem or prose piece that describes some aspect of water. They return back to the group and read poems.

A brief outline for the class:

- Each day opens with a water poem from poets such as Emerson, Whitman, Goethe, Frost, Rilke, Muir, Cothell

- Review the following concepts to inform the writing: watershed, aquifer, wetland, water table, biodiversity, ground water, gray water and black water, head waters and outflow

- Study legends and histories of ancient cultures in relationship to water

- Students create "word banks" that will inspire poetry writing. A "word bank" is a deposit of many words that focus on a topic. Their "word banks" have to do with a deeper understanding of the ecology of water. For example: shoreline, erosion, flood, drought, rivulet, watershed, dripping, etc.

- Students may take words from the "word bank" in writing their poetry. This gives a starting point and can stimulate creative ideas

- Introduce the concept and process of Goethean observation to the students, then go out to sit in nature. This deep observation develops new tools for hearing and seeing nature in an objective way. This can lead the students to creativity in their writing. Goethean observation means being with something in nature and allowing a variety of objective insights to facilitate a flow of information that is communicated to the self from the object of observation in a meditative way. This leads from discreet observations such as, the bark is brown, to a sense for the wholeness of the tree. Through this process likes and dislikes are left out in order to let the tree speak, allowing the thought to arrive without a self-generated thinking process. By stilling the personal feelings they can become one with what they are observing

- Students develop a "sense of place" by exploring nature ecology in their writing themes and experiences. This is facilitated by the exercise of inhabiting a particular place over time, becoming familiar with its physical properties and getting to know its history. Students explore their place in relationship to their own personal history and where they feel at home or have a sense of belonging

- Each day has a particular water theme introduced through reading a poem from an established poet that relates to the topic. For homework each night the students write a poem inspired by the reading. These poems are shared the next day in class

- The culmination of the block is a poetry reading where each student contributes their best poems

Farm Economics (Year-Round)

What you will need:

- Rulers; paper; colored pencils; pens

What to do:

Develop a model for the students to work through from a real or imagined situation. If using an imagined model, ask the students to construct their ideal farm with a water source, crops, animals, housing, utilities and markets, and a specific number of owners. They can also take one aspect of a working farm and look at income and output of that aspect. In the classroom they draw a farm to scale, put in all the elements, create a scale and key, and create a farm budget. Another project to explore is having the students create a product themselves that can be sold at the school fair or farmstand as a real model, such as raising ducks for eggs, growing cut flowers, or making an herbal product.

Bridge Building (Year-Round)

What you will need:

- Wood; nails or screws; a cordless drill; level; handsaw; lumber

What to do:

Swales necessitate bridges so that humans can cross. Bridges must be sturdy enough to carry wheelbarrows of material. They can be made from thick plywood or assembled with slats on a base. This can be a solitary project or two students working together. The students can be left to figure it out and consult with the teacher as needed. Each bridge reflects the unique style and thinking of the individual student.

FALL PROJECTS

Erosion Control (Fall)

What you will need:

- A-frame levels (can make yourself); shovels; wheelbarrows; landscape flags; weed blocker fabric or burlap; U-stakes; hammers or small sledge hammers

What to do:

Erosion control can take many forms particular to your property. A simple form of erosion control can be cover cropping in the winter. If the land or garden has a slope, then swales or ditches can be dug to catch water by slowing, spreading and stopping water from carrying the topsoil to the bottom of the hill.

Using an A-frame level, have the students identify the peak and sides of the slope and mark this with at least five landscape flags. Find a high point and extension from that point within an uncultivated area or near the upper perimeter of the garden. Dig trenches that follow the contour of the slope or the slope itself, to guide the water to an intended place. The swale can be one to two feet wide and one to two feet deep. Swales that follow a slope can be lined with fabric and rocks to create a dry creek bed. Swales on contour drain slowly and may not need to be lined. Berms are created from the soil dug out to create the swale and should be located downslope from the swale, but can be on both sides.

This is hard work that really meets the students and it is surprising how much pleasure they get from digging deep. The archetypal action of water moving on land resonates with the movement of their blood in veins and arteries. In the winter we investigate how well the swales are functioning and make necessary changes.

Nature Trails (Fall)

See "Map & Build a Nature Trail" (p. 134). Tenth grade is a wonderful time to bring back this activity with students that are are more capable of planning, directing, and executing the project.

Cob Construction (Fall)

Cob construction is an ancient form of building that is useful for making wood-fired ovens, walls, and benches. Either construct a roof for your structure prior to building it, or be prepared to do annual maintenance and repair.

What you will need:

*   Clay soil; sand; straw or fresh manure; water; shovels; wheelbarrows; a tarp and bare-feet (masonry troughs or cement mixer are optional); oil and pigments for final plaster layer

What to do:

Building with cob is a great social, community-building activity. Handling materials that come right from the earth is very engaging and exciting for the students. It empowers their sense of self-sufficiency. The process of building with cob involves mixing sand, straw, and clay soil in specific proportions depending on your soil. Students mix the ingredients with their feet on a tarp, adding water, to get the texture correct. A base for the structure, made of urbanite, large rocks, or bricks must be formed prior to cobbing. Cob structures are built by layering handfuls of this "adobe" mixture upon each other to form up the walls. The surfaces of the walls are smoothed until the desired shape is achieved. It is physically demanding and slow going and uses local resources, which makes it inexpensive and artistic. Have one group mix, and once the first batch is ready, the other group applies the cob, while more cob is being mixed to keep the process going. The students take turns stomping and adding ingredients to the mixture. A good plan for clean up is needed at the end of each work session. The teacher should have a well thought out plan to implement the project through to the final finishes and necessary weatherproofing. Otherwise, the work will melt away in the rain. Kiko Denzer's book *Build Your Own Earth Oven* is an excellent primer.

Winter Projects

Grafting Fruit Trees (Winter)

What you will need:

- Grafting knives; rubber bands; grafting tape; metal plant tags; pruners; rootstocks; scion wood; pots and potting soil; first aid kit

What to do:

Consult a tutorial on bench grafting to familiarize yourself with the process. Master Gardener programs or Rare Fruit Grower Societies are a great resource for scion wood and instruction.

This is an activity that needs extreme caution and supervision. Graft with no more than five students at a time. Gather at a picnic table or worktable for the work. All safety precautions are explained at the beginning, as grafting knives are extremely sharp. Demonstrate cutting into the rootstock to split the base for the cleft graft and then show the slicing of the scion wood. The matching of the cambium on at least one side of the scion and the receiving rootstock must line up perfectly, before wrapping with the rubber bands and grafting tape. Label loosely with a metal tag and pot up. The students may plant them in the garden after the cuttings show that the grafts have been successful (at least two to three months later).

Perennial Pruning (Winter)

What you will need:

- Pruners and wheelbarrows

What to do:

Perennial pruning can be taught on fruit trees, roses, berries, or any other herbaceous perennial plant. Train students to see plant growth in relationship to time, using terms like old wood, new wood, and fruitwood. This leads to an ability to guide the plant in its future growth by removing material at a certain node in relationship to the shape of the plant and the bearing of fruit or cut flowers. Teach the student to recognize the correct place to cut through practice and repetition. In the beginning, students can ask if it is correct before they cut. After reassurance they can cut on their own. Pairing students to consult with each other can help them gain confidence. The last step is to remove any suckers at the bottom of the plant and gather all prunings to take to the compost or burn pile.

Eleventh Grade *"WHY ARE PEOPLE SUFFERING AND HOW CAN I BE OF SERVICE?"*

The eleventh grade student can now synthesize inner ideals with wider world issues. They have a social consciousness and an ability to be empathetic. Polarities have been resolved. As their sense of self grows stronger they are able to use these strengths and capacities in social situations with people in need. They are now able to be self-directed in their learning and their work, taking up tasks with ownership and intention.

Connecting With The Classroom Curriculum

Microcosmic studies in biology (looking at cells) are balanced with macrocosmic studies of the biosphere and ecology in the classroom. Epic questions raised through reading *Parzival* bring discussions about the meaning of life and of suffering. Their work in plant propagation is supported by their new understanding of cell development and of growth patterns gained in their classroom studies.

Social Dynamics

Social conscience awakens the ability to have empathy for the "other." Politics and economics are discussed with maturity. With their sense of self in place they are less dependent on their friendships to give them a sense of belonging in the world. This gives them the ability to look at the needs of others rather than being preoccupied with their own needs. Their self-confidence gives them an ability to bring their will to tasks of service. Class dynamics stabilize as the students stand more firmly in themselves. Students start to think about college, yet they are not as weighed down by it as the twelfth grader: they are looking towards college with excitement rather than stress.

Eleventh Grade Gardening Curriculum Overview

Goals:

- Students gain an ability to work on complex social and ethical issues
- Students can apply themselves in self-directed learning projects
- Students feel motivated and empowered through their insights

Key Skills:

- Through sustainable farming practices students are able to grow healthy food for themselves and for the community
- Students participate in the tasks of gardening without resistance
- Students are aware of how their contribution serves the community
- Rather than simply complying with the task of the moment, they can see the project in its totality and take responsibility on their own initiative
- Thinking, feeling, and willing finally come into harmony with each other: they are physically capable of the task, they can think through the necessary steps, and they care about the outcome

Primary Activities for Eleventh Grade

In a classroom setting, investigate the global picture of agriculture within world culture and economics. What are the circumstances behind poverty and hunger? What are the effects of pesticides? Is genetic engineering safe? Is globalization helpful? Are corporations ethical? The students look at themselves in relationship to the issues of our time. To quote Julia Butterfly Hill, "We live in challenging times that are calling each of us to step into life as service. Hope does not exist in the ethers; it comes alive only in the space of our committed action." A useful resource is the book, *Hope's Edge* by Francis Moore Lappe, which gives viable solutions and examples of resourceful communities coming together to solve problems in innovative ways. It is important to have hopeful solutions following an exploration of our contemporary world problems. The most creative solutions come out of the greatest adversity.

This study shows us that through sustainable farming practices, the students can grow healthy food, build community, and see their true relationship to nature and their present opportunity to give back and not just to take. The practical work on the farm gives them the skills and the confidence to be an agrarian, if they choose, or to value those who are.

Outside, they are engaged in all the tasks of the farm: planting, weeding, mulching, and composting. It is in the work that the concepts come alive. In the garden the work is familiar, yet it takes on new significance as they explore the complex issues in the world today. Now the students can face these challenges with insight and consciousness.

Curriculum Examples

YEAR-ROUND PROJECTS

Food & Farming Research Project (Year-Round)

What you will need:

- Resource binders or bibliographies containing resources on a variety of topics that the students might want to explore in depth.

What to do:

Ask the students to research a specific topic and present it back to the class. Their work should be analytical and specific. Suggested topics include: urban vs. rural agriculture; recycling; eco-economics; fair trade & fair wages; permaculture; health and nutrition; chemicals and pesticides; the clothing industry. Students can work in groups and make a presentation to the class that is both visual and oral.

Fall Projects

Plant Propagation (Fall)

Plants propagated by the eleventh grade can be sold as a fundraiser, shared with other gardening classes or donated to schools that don't have a greenhouse. This class is appropriate for any age high school student and is best structured as an ongoing class so the students can see the developmental stages and be there for the next task.

What you will need:

- A propagation area or greenhouse; propagation mix ingredients; plant flats and pots; softwood plant cuttings; sifting screen; wheelbarrows; shovels; pruners; plastic nursery pots and trays; round shovels; popsicle sticks; wooden plant tags or old Levolor blinds cut into pieces for plant labels

What to do:

Annual Seedling Propagation

Every class does seeding as needed on a rotating basis. In eleventh grade, greenhouse seeding is one of four propagation practices they do. They are very familiar with this task from previous years.

Propagation by Softwood Cuttings

To create more plants, take cuttings from perennial plants, and insert them into a soilless medium of perlite and vermiculite or sand until they form new roots. By keeping them hydrated beneath the soil, the node uses its growth forces to make roots. Each cutting needs to contain two or three nodes. Take cuttings from flexible, supple growth without mature blossoms. Strip off the leaves on the bottom nodes and cut the stem below the bottom node. The tip should only contain about two sets of leaves. Place your propagation mix in an open flat or pots and moisten. Poke holes with a pencil. Insert the cuttings and firm the mix around the stem. Plants become dependent on humans when they are in containers, so daily watering is absolutely necessary. A plastic dome can also help to maintain moisture.

The willow plant is the easiest to reproduce by cuttings, as it contains within itself rooting hormones, and the success rate with this plant is the greatest. In appropriate climates, the next most successful cutting is the fig. With a sturdy stem and many nodes, it maintains vitality. Lavender is another plant that seems to do well as a cutting. Once the cuttings have well-established root systems and new leaf growth, the students can transplant them into potting soil and later into the garden.

Propagation by Layering

Propagate strawberries by catching the runners in small pots of soil in place in the garden, letting them root, and then cutting them away from the mother plant and planting them elsewhere. Small irrigation stakes are helpful to keep the runner plants in place in the pots.

Propagation by Division

Clusters of garden plants that are too close to each other or have gotten too large, such as bulbs, rhizomes, and stolens can be divided and repotted or replanted elsewhere in the garden. Other plants with stable roots such as berries or Echinacea can be lifted and carefully divided.

Seed Saving (Fall and Winter)

What you will need:

- Jars or envelopes; markers; small and large bowls; sifting screens in graduated sizes (optional); clippers; buckets or wheelbarrows; a tarp for threshing

What to do:

Seed saving is an important activity to ensure next year's crop. At this age it is appropriate to cover the science of seed saving as well as the practice. Students carefully gather seeds from flowers, herbs, vegetables and grains. Depending on the quantity to gather, use bowls, buckets or wheelbarrows to gather in seeds or whole dried plants. Remove mature seed heads with clippers. Then help the student identify the seed compared to other parts of the seed head. After gathering, the next step is threshing, which can be done gently with your hands and fingers or more rigorously on a tarp with feet. Wheat, beans and brassicas are suitable for the tarp method. The goal is to separate the seed from the plant. Next is winnowing away the remaining chaff. Techniques include sifting, blowing, using a fan while tossing seeds in the air or pouring them from one container to another, or removing debris by hand. The final phase is to carefully package and label the seeds. With jars, there can be no moisture in the jar and the seeds must be fully dried. Seeds are stored in a cool and dark environment. Seed saving reminds us of nature's abundance and allows us to share and exchange seeds with others.

Deadheading (Fall)

What you will need:

- Pruners

What to do:

The eleventh grader is much more discerning and can readily practice the skill of deadheading which they began to practice in fifth grade. The lesson goes deeper now, as they are able to see not just the node, but also the different developmental stages that are present on the plant simultaneously as the blossoms and seed heads mature. By questioning the student, they begin to look deeply and see the different growth stages: Which is the youngest bud on the plant? Which is the oldest? Find all the variable stages in between. Then they begin to see how incredibly unique each plant's growth is. The deadheading is the final deed once they can see the importance of taking away the old growth to enhance the growth of the new. They begin to see the mystery of plant development.

Twelfth Grade "Self Knowledge Becomes Rightful Action"

Twelfth grade students need to see real answers to real problems. They want to work with specialists and go deeper into topics that they are interested in. Week long internships can solidify these experiences and also link with their senior thesis project. With their hard won knowledge and experience, a high school senior can be a model and mentor for others and is a strong example in their school community. Given the opportunity they will shine. It is a time to integrate the years of previous study with the awakened self and take this knowledge and independence into a chosen field of study or work.

Connecting With The Classroom Curriculum

In the twelfth grade, students bring all parts of the curriculum together to create an overview. In the sciences, they take up biochemistry in both the qualitative and quantitative approach. Chemistry and physics are investigated through phenomenology. In art classes, the "self" is in focus in both the self-portrait and the clay bust. Through these art projects they must observe their face, notice its proportions, and depict it as accurately as possible. The student must continually reexamine who they are and how they see themselves. The twelfth grader is ready to be launched. Because their study has become so rich and full, they have many resources to call on. They are independent and able to choose farming projects that they are clearly motivated to pursue and complete. Making the world a better place to live and having the skills for independence is an impetus towards practical application of all previous skills.

Social Dynamics

The student must find the balance between their individualization and their deeds in the world. Their strong individuality helps them to work harmoniously with fellow students and teachers. Their ideas and deeds must be truly self-determined. Now the initiation of their interests and tasks that they take up come from within. By following this truth they can have compassion and acceptance for the same process taking form in their fellow students. In order for the group to be healthy, each individual must be following their path. If this self-development hasn't happened, social conflict more appropriate to ninth grade can manifest in the twelfth grade class.

TWELFTH GRADE GARDENING CURRICULUM OVERVIEW

Goals:

- Students can manage a large amount of freedom
- The teacher becomes a resource and support while the student takes the lead

- By being given freedom students shine as strong individuals.

Key Skills:
- Ability to mentor younger students
- Self-managed work, research and focus
- Independently conceiving of and implementing a special project that serves the school community and relates to the big picture of ecology and farming
- Taking responsibility for what they leave behind as their legacy

Primary Activities for Twelfth Grade

YEAR-ROUND PROJECTS

Independent Projects (Year-Round)

What to do:

Give students an opportunity to choose a project that benefits the garden or school or the greater community. The scope of the project must be significant and this can be accomplished by giving a time frame, for example, twelve hours broken down to one hour each week for twelve weeks. Weekly check-ins help to keep the students on track and provide the needed resources. Sometimes the teacher must find other specialists to assist or mentor a particular student. Usually the project itself becomes visible to the community in a physical form. Some examples of projects include building a solar panel to generate an electric water pump to move water from rainwater catchment, designing and illustrating a field-guide for the plants and insects in the campus garden, or educating the community about toxins and chemicals in makeup through making and selling natural products at the winter fair.

Building Redwood Seeding Flats (Year-Round)

What you will need:
- Redwood bender board (1-inch by 3-inch); fine nails; hammer; saw

What to do:

Seedlings in flats have a better opportunity to grow a healthy root structure than in individual plastic pots where they are quickly root bound. Flats can be reused over and over in the greenhouse as opposed to plastic pots and trays, which eventually crack and break. The finished flat should be 14 inches wide, 23 inches long, and 3 ¼ inches deep. Cut laterals and attach end boards on the outside with fine nails. Slats cover the bottom with ⅛ inch space between each slat.

Supporting Other School Gardens (Year-Round)

What to do:

Reach out and make contact with a school in your community that needs help developing their school garden program. Find one teacher at the school to serve as a liaison with your students. In the beginning this also demands your help to facilitate the logistics and communication, until the program has evolved to a point where processes and practices are in place that allow the students to take leadership. Often, this kind of work necessitates grant writing or fundraising for garden building materials. Building a new garden at a sister school involves site planning and development in collaboration with the teacher. The teacher often develops the curriculum and the seniors help implement it by working with the younger students in the garden. Many schools have state standards that must be met and the teacher knows best how to incorporate them. Once the program has a successful year, a senior student or two can take up the work more easily the following year. Workdays for special building projects can even involve younger high school students under the seniors' direction. Similar service projects could be implemented in community gardens or on farms in need of help.

Creek Cleanup & Restoration (Year-Round)

What to do:

Contact the local City or County Water Department. There is usually someone who manages trash removal events to clean up the watershed or creeks. This could also involve removing invasive plants as well as planting plants to mitigate erosion. You can either coordinate with an already planned cleanup day or create a school workday with a group of students. The agency coordinates the cleanup plan, brings the materials, and hauls the trash. Teachers should supervise their students.

Recycle Awareness (Year-Round)

What you need:

- Construct or purchase labeled recycling containers that are a different color than the garbage containers, as well as small compost containers for all the garbage collection areas on campus.

What to do:

Twelfth graders are well suited for ensuring that recycling actually happens at your school. Form a "Green Team" that meets weekly to explore the practices, education, communication and logistics that must happen to bring awareness to the proper habits of recycling. The "Green Team" should consist of a teacher and at least six or more students. If you have a groundsperson or agreeable facilities maintenance staff, include them in the introductory meeting(s). If not, a system will need to be created for students to collect and sort materials. In the introductory meetings, share ideas and have someone take notes. Begin to implement the ideas through school assemblies, announcements, and signage. Good methods of education include skits, relay races, films, and guest speakers. The team continues with monitoring, mentoring, and educating, as this is an ongoing project. As people dispose of waste, a lot of mistakes are made that must be sorted out at the end of the day when the garbage is collected.

Ecological Issues (Year-Round)

What to do:

Ecological issues can be made visible to the students through films, guest speakers, collaboration on community projects, extended field-trips, habitat protection, and attendance at regional meetings or conferences. For example, a seminar and discussion on climate change is a place where students can research and gather information and share strategies on this currently evolving topic. After screening a film or hearing a panel, breakout discussion groups help to integrate and process what they have heard.

Set up further projects and participation around the issue so that they are engaged in their will and not just their thinking. Change takes action and talk is cheap. The teacher helps to facilitate the students finding their areas of interest in order that they are able to bring their ideas to fruition. It is healthy for students to choose one problem to sort out and find solutions for, rather than being overwhelmed by a forest of difficulties. By staying involved and engaged they have a perspective that's more positive.

Fall Projects

Native Plant Garden (Fall)

What you will need:

- An area of land in which to create a hedgerow or garden for growing native plants; native plants; compost; irrigation system; plant labels; shovels; wheelbarrows

What to do:

This project helps to reestablish those plants that were here before, and can provide important habitats for insects, pollinators, and wildlife. The first thing to do is research with the students which plants are native to your area. There is often a native plant society that can be a resource both with information and plant purchasing. It's important to know the height and width that each plant will achieve and incorporate this into your planting design. Consider how humans will interact with this area and whether there will need to be signage, paths, benches, water feature, etc. Sometimes invasive plants and weeds need to be removed first after pre-irrigating. Be watchful for poisonous plants, which are often in undeveloped areas. Thoroughly examine the site before removing anything, as there might already be native plants in the area.

Bibliography

Waldorf Education

Glas, Norbert. *Conception, Birth and Early Childhood.* Spring Valley, NY: Anthroposophic Press, 1983.

Howard, Michael. *Educating the Will.* Chatham, NY: Waldorf Publications, 2015.

Kovacs, Charles. *Botany.* Edinburgh: Floris Books, 2005.

Krause, Rudolf. Trans. Gisela and Nicholas Franceschelli. *Gardening Classes at the Waldorf Schools.* Kimberton, PA: Bio-Dynamic Farming and Gardening Association, 1992.

Rawson, Martin, and Kevin Avison. *The Tasks and Content of the Steiner-Waldorf Curriculum.* Edinburgh: Floris Books, 2014.

Schoorel, Edmond. *The First Seven Years: Physiology of Childhood.* Fair Oaks: Rudolf Steiner College Press, 2004.

Steiner, Rudolf. *The Education of the Child.* Great Barrington, MA: Anthroposophic Press, 1996.

Steiner, Rudolf. *Study of Man.* Forest Row: Rudolf Steiner Press, 1981.

Steiner, Rudolf. *Soul Economy.* Great Barrington, MA: Anthroposophic Press, 2003.

Agriculture

Astyk, Sharon and Aaron Newton. *A Nation of Farmers.* Gabriola Island, B.C.: New Society Publishers. 2009.

Bell, Graham. *The Permaculture Garden.* Hammersmith: Thorsons, 1994.

Carpenter, Novella and Willow Rosenthal. *The Essential Urban Farmer.* London: Penguin Books. 2011.

Hemenway, Toby. *Gaia's Garden: A Guide to Home Scale Permaculture*. White River Junction, VT: Chelsea Green, 2000.

Hill, Lewis. *Secrets of Plant Propagation: Starting Your Own Flowers, Vegetables, Fruits, Berries, Shrubs, Trees and Houseplants*. Pownal: Storey Communications, 1985.

Jeavons , John. *How to Grow More Vegetables*. 6th ed. Ten Speed Press, 2004

Kimbrell, Andrew. *The Fatal Harvest Reader: The Tragedy of Industrial Agriculture*. Sausalito: Foundations of Deep Ecology, 2002.

Lappe, Frances Moore and Anna Lappe. *Hope's Edge: The Next Diet for a Small Planet*. New York: Tarcher-Putnam, 2002.

Lanza, Patricia. *Lasagna Gardening*. Emmaus, PA: Rodale Press. 1998.

Mars, Ross. *The Basics of Permaculture Design*. White River Junction: Chelsea Green, 2005.

Morrow, Joel. *Vegetable Gardening for Organic and Biodynamic Growers*. Great Barrington, MA: SteinerBooks, 2014.

Philbrick, Helen and Richard Gregg. *Companion Plants and How to Use Them*. Edinburgh: Floris Books, 2016.

Steiner, Rudolf. *Agriculture*. Kimberton: Bio-Dynamic Farming and Gardening Association, 1993.

Storl, Wolf D. *Culture and Horticulture*. Berkeley, CA: North Atlantic Books, 2013.

Environmental & Outdoor Education

Ausubel, Kenny with J.P. Harpignies. *Nature's Operating Instructions: The True Biotechnologies*. San Francisco: Sierra Club Books, 2004.

Bieber, Ed. *What Color Is The Wind? A FEEL Guide to the Out-of-doors for Parents with Young Children*. Nature Place Publishing, 2012.

Cornell, Josheph Bharat. *Sharing Nature With Children*. Nevada City: Ananda Publications, 1979.

Chesman, Andrea, ed. *The Big Book of Gardening Skills*. Pownal: Story Communications, 1993.

Denzer, Kiko and Hannah Field. *Build Your Own Earth Oven.* Blodgett, OR: Hand Print Press, 2007.

Diehn, Gwen, and Terry Krautwurst. *Nature Crafts for Kids: 50 Fantastic Things To Make With Mother Nature's Help.* New York: Sterling, 1992.

Dobson, Clive, and Gregor Gilpin Beck. *Watersheds: A Practical Handbook for Healthy Water.* Buffalo: Firefly Books, 1999.

Dunks, Tom, and Patty. *Gardening With Children.* Santa Cruz: Harvest Press, 1976.

Elpel, Thomas J. *Botany in a Day: The Patterns Method of Plant Identification.* Pony, MT: Hops Press, 2004.

Fell, Derek. *A Kid's First Book of Gardening: Growing Plants: Growing Plants Indoors and Out.* Philadelphia: Running Press, 1989.

Fromherz, Andrea, and Edith Biderman. *The Wonder of Trees: Nature Activities for Children.* Edinburgh: Floris Books, 2012.

Funk, Alicia, and Karin Kaufman. *Living Wild: Gardening, Cooking and Healing with Native Plants for the Sierra Nevada.* Nevada City: Flicker Press, 2012.

Holdredge, Craig. *Thinking Like a Plant: A Living Science for Life.* Great Barrington: Lindisfarne Books, 2013.

Kimmerer, Robyn Wall. *Braiding Sweet Grass: Indigenous Wisdom, Scientific Knowledge, and the Teachings of Plants.* Minneapolis: Milkweed Editions, 2013.

Kowalchik, Clair & William H. Hylton, eds. *Rodale's Illustrated Encyclopedia of Herbs.* Emmaus: Rodale Press. 1987.

Louv, Richard. *Last Child in the Woods: Saving our Children from Nature Deficit Disorder.* Chapel Hill: Algonquin Books, 2008.

Petrash, Carol. *Earthways: Simple Environmental Activities for Young Children.* Mt. Rainier, WA: Gryphon House, 1992.

Pranis, Eve, and Amy Gifford. *Growing Ventures: Starting a School Garden Business.* So. Burlington: National Gardening Association, 2003.

Russell, George K. *Children and Nature: Making Connections.* Great Barrington: The Myrin Institute, 2014.

Stone, Michael K. *Smart by Nature: Schooling for Sustainability*. Healdsburg: Watershed Media, 2009.

Stone, Michael K and Zenobia Barlow. *Ecological Literacy: Educating our Children for a Sustainable World*. San Francisco: Sierra Club Books. 2005.

Sustainable World Coalition. *Sustainable World Source Book*. Berkeley: Sustainable World Coalition, 2014.

Tierra, Leslie. *A Kid's Herb Book for Children of All Ages*. Brandon: Robert D. Reed Publishers, 2000.

U.C. Cooperative Extension. *TWIGS: Youth Development Program*. Half Moon Bay: U.C. Cooperative Extension, 1997.

Vollmer, Mason. *Growing Gardens/Growing People*. Blevens Press, 2015.

Wilkinson, Roy. *Studies in Practical Activities: Farming, Gardening, Housebuilding*. Sussex: Rudolf Steiner Education, 1975.

Stories for Students

Aliki. *Corn Is Maize: The Gift of the Indians*. HarperCollins, 1986.

Brown, Marcia. *Stone Soup*. Aladdin, 1997.

Caduto, Michael and Joseph Bruchac. *Keepers of Life: Discovering Plants Through Native American Stories and Earth Activities*. Golden: Fulcrum Publishing, 1994.

Denee, Joanne. *In the Three Sister's Garden: American Stories and Seasonal Activities for the Curious Child*. Montpelier: Common Roots Press, 1995.

Giono, Jean. *The Man Who Planted Trees*. White River Junction: Chelsea Green, 2007.

Poer, Nancy Jewel. *Mia's Apple Tree*. Placerville: White Feather Publishing, 2004.

Roads, Dorothy. *The Corn Grows Ripe*. Puffin Books, 1993.

Poetry, Verse, & Song

Lebret, Elizabeth. *Pentatonic Songs*. Toronto: Waldorf Assoc. of Ontario, 1985.

Middleton, Julie Forest. *Songs for Earthlings: A Green Spirituality Songbook*. Philadelphia: Emerald Earth Publishing, 1998.

Poulsson, Emilie. *Fingerplays for Nursery and Kindergarten*. Mineola, NY: Dover Publications, 2011.

Roth, Chris. *The Beetless' Gardening Book*. Cottage Grove: Carrotseed Press, 1997.

Spring; Summer; Autumn; and *Winter*. Stourbridge: Wynstones Press, 1999.

ENVIRONMENTAL, EDUCATIONAL, & AGRICULTURAL ORGANIZATIONS

The Biodyamic Association (BDA)	\<biodynamics.com\>
The California School Garden Network	\<www.csgn.org\>
Center for Ecoliteracy	\<ecoliteracy.org\>
The Children and Nature Network	\<childrenandnature.org\>
The Edible Schoolyard Network	\<edibleschoolyard.org\>
Farm Based Education Network	\<farmbasededucation.org\>
Farm Based Educators Inspired by Anthroposophy	\<biodynamics.com/fbeiba\>
National Gardening Association	\<garden.org\>
Native Seeds/SEARCH (NS/S)	\<nativeseeds.org\>
Natural Start Alliance	\<naturalstart.org\>
North American Association of Environmental Education	\<naaee.org\>
Seed Savers Exchange	\<seedsavers.org\>

Index

ACKNOWLEDGEMENTS

We are ever grateful to Gene Gollogly for his interest in our book and John Scott Legg for his editorial assistance. Miguel Salmerow generously provided beautiful photos of Summerfield Waldorf School and Farm—thank you Miguel!

From Ronni: Many thanks to Alan York and Hilmar Moore for instruction on how to be a Biodynamic farmer. Thank you to Perry Hart and Mason Volmer for opening the gates to Summerfield Waldorf School and Farm; Gunther Hauk for answering my questions and being a wonderful "garden teacher mentor"; Fentress Gardener for sharing his work at Hawthorne Valley School and inspiring the development my own curriculum.

From Willow: Thank you Ronni for inviting me to work with and learn from you—this experience has given me the deep drink of water I needed when I was thirsting for a way to advance a field of work I care about deeply. I am grateful to Harald and Cynthia Hoven for teaching me the theory and practice of biodynamic farming. Thank you to my Fellowship and Apprenticeship students, and my preschool students for allowing me to share my love of biodynamic farming and hone my teaching skills. I will be ever grateful to Dorit Winter for providing a solid foundation in anthroposophy and Waldorf education. Finally, I give thanks to Rudolf Steiner for transmitting the wisdom that has allowed me to find a hopeful and purposeful direction through biodynamic farming and Waldorf pedagogy.

We give thanks to our readers, Leslie Loy, Carol Nimick, and Tom Van Gorden, whose thoughtful, careful reading and suggestions have helped to make this book so much better.

—Ronni Sands & Willow Summer

Ronni Sands has been a Waldorf Garden Teacher at Summerfield Waldorf School and Farm near Santa Rosa, California for more than twenty years. She has also worked as a Waldorf kindergarten teacher, a market gardener, a landscaper, and a house parent for handicapped adults on a farm. Today she teaches high school students gardening, cooking, basket weaving, herbal studies, and sustainability. Her work in environmental studies and garden teaching have inspired a long line of graduates who take this work out into the world, many of whom have become gardening teachers themselves.

Willow Summer has been gardening and farming since she first learned to plant a corn patch with her father at age four. After college she moved to the Bay Area where she founded the non-profit urban farming program City Slicker Farms, which grew from one empty lot garden in 2000 to seven urban farms and a Backyard Garden Building Program supplying thousands of pounds of urban-grown organic produce each year. Willow went on to start The Berkeley Basket, an urban community supported agriculture farm. In 2011 she co-authored *The Essential Urban Farmer* (Penguin Books; with Novella Carpenter) and received a teaching certificate from the Bay Area Center for Waldorf Teacher Training with the goal of inspiring children and adults through farm and garden education.